Living With a Rock Star and a Super Hero

Creating a new normal with Down Syndrome
and Sensory Processing Disorder.

Amie L. Merz

Moving Mountains Motivations
©2015

Table of Contents

Introduction

We have a son with Down Syndrome. It's not "Downs" Syndrome, or "Downs", and he's not a "retard". Down Syndrome, or DS, is a condition named after John Langdon Down who researched cranium size of his patients and ultimately realized the physical similarities of the DS population. Down Syndrome is a common chromosomal abnormality that cannot be caused or prevented, but one pregnancy that is often terminated, if parents discover the abnormality during genetic testing.

We didn't know he had DS before he was born, and we knew very little about the diagnosis until we **had** to learn it. It is one of those things that you don't really think will happen to you. We all know something difficult can happen at any time in life, but you just don't know what or when. This we were not prepared for, but we pulled together as a family and now barely remember a time before Ben. If we had known the diagnosis during my pregnancy, nothing would be different today except our preparation and knowledge about the disability before he was born.

I am aware of the ignorance and discrimination regarding people with DS. I hear it; I've seen it. The negativity, the rude slurs. And yet, in his ten years, people have given him more love and affection than I would have ever expected. You know when people see a newborn in the grocery store and feel like they can smile, or coo, or talk to the baby, even though they are strangers? That is how it is with kids with Down Syndrome their whole lives. People talk to Ben, greet Ben, give him gifts. He's ten, but it's like having a newborn, where people say, "Oh he's so cute, how old is he?"

This especially became evident to me when I started using Facebook years ago. Ben can do some funny and crazy things, so he is often the subject of my status updates. What has surprised me is the number of people who come up to me in person and say, "Oh I just love your stories about Ben! Keep 'em coming." Someone I barely know will say, "Oh, so and so told me about that thing Ben did the other day!" He apparently precedes himself.

These encounters inspired me to write the "Ben stories" down in a central location, hence this book. I'm sure there are some good ones I've forgotten, and I know that Ben could probably tell the stories better himself, and would relish the opportunity. But for now, this is what I've got. This kid is a hoot. He is a handful and an attention seeker, and yet his ingenuity surprises and prides us every day. This book is my way of sharing the magic of Ben with those who don't have the honor of living with him.

As a disclaimer, this is only our account, our understanding and our experience with Down Syndrome. Every kid and every family is different, and what has been effective or typical for us may not be so for another family with DS. We have done a lot of research; but more often than not, we fly by the seat of our pants and hope it works. Sometimes it does, sometimes not. This book was written for entertainment, not as a guide for raising a child with DS. There are better ways to do it than we have done. But what we do have is love, humor, creativity, and a great bunch of family and friends surrounding us in support.

There was a recent study alluding to the future possibility of a "cure" for Down Syndrome. So theoretically, if we could take away this extra chromosome and the traits that go with it, would we? That's a tough call. Ben has the most unique personality, presence, and energy. We would love for Ben to have every opportunity that kids without disabilities have. And yet, is there some benefit to being Ben? He thinks so. We think so. He's a rock star.

Chapter One
To C or Not to C (section)

People often tell the story of the moment time stood still — the event when their lives changed forever into the "Before" and the "After": what their life was like before the event, and how it was forever changed after. Of course you never know you are going to have those life-changing moments in advance — the minute something happens that will alter your course in such a way that in retrospect you remember it forever. You and the person you share it with are eternally connected by something intangible that no one else would ever understand. Memories of that moment make you look at the person across the room, connect eyes without words, both of you just knowing…the significance of that minute.

Tony and I thought we had already had that moment. In 2000 our son Lucas was born after a very healthy pregnancy but a very stressful birth. My water broke at 8:00 on a Wednesday morning, when I was getting ready to go to a routine doctor visit. I remember standing in my dining room, thinking, *Oh that's gonna stain the carpet!* (Ew right?) But I didn't have any contractions. So I called the doctor to see if I should come to my scheduled appointment, but they said go to the hospital. I called Tony, who was already at work, to tell him the news. We live in the boonies. The woods. Far away from "town". So for him to come an hour home from work and then drive me an hour back to the hospital — not practical. So I said I'd meet him at his office.

Nine-plus months pregnant, water leaking, alone, an hour from town, sure I'll drive myself. What could go wrong? But… I can be a bit stubborn at times so I did it. Probably not the wisest decision, but considering Lucas wasn't born until 38 hours later, it turned out fine.

After minimal contractions or dilation, the hospital staff "induced" me, giving me Pitocin to start the process. By 5:00 am on Thursday, the pain was unbearable; but I had not dilated far enough to get an epidural, and I started vomiting. Family visiting, staff checking my no-longer private area, me vomiting: what could be more fun? How about an anesthesiologist trying to give me an epidural but giving me a spinal-block instead? This caused there to be no feeling from the waist down. Nurses and aides had to move my legs for me, humiliating, and then… my blood pressure tanked. You've never seen people scurry so fast, getting me an epinephrine shot (I think that's what it was, who knows at that point?) and checking the baby's heart rate.

Tony was scared out of his mind. He is a big tough guy 99.9% of the time, but in this moment he was powerless and afraid. He later said that was the deciding factor for him, almost losing us, and he didn't want us to get pregnant again. This experience had already been too stressful and he didn't want to risk that again. Little did we know what the future had in store for us.

Eventually, still puking, not feeling my legs, my doctor agreed to do a C-section, and I was thrilled. What a strange thing a C-section is. Being awake while they cut you open, feeling the tugs while they move body parts around.

Tony was able to watch while sitting next to my head, and he said they laid my organs out on my stomach to get to the baby. What?! They did what? All the while the doctors and nurses chatted about the latest novel they were reading. I remember trying to add my two cents about the book they were discussing, but maybe that was just in my mind.

After all of that, Lucas came out perfectly. They took Tony with him to the nursery, where he took more pictures and learned how to bathe and feed him. Because my blood pressure had been wonky, they gave me magnesium sulfate to stabilize, which made me puke. And they gave me morphine, which made me puke. So for the first 24 hours of my new baby's life, Tony took very good care of him, and I threw up. There is a cute picture of my friend Lisa holding baby Lucas, and in the background, me puking. In retrospect, it's funny. At the time, not so much.

Four years later, when pregnant with Ben, I had the option of either having another scheduled C-section or what they call VBAC (vaginal birth after C-section). They said I could choose. Tough call! On the one hand I wanted the excitement of "going into labor." On the other, I like control, and planning the date was tempting. I asked everyone I knew what they thought, but the deciding factor came when chatting with my doctor's partner, and he mentioned, "Well, after C-sections, you won't have the same vaginal trauma and so might not have as many incontinence issues later." SOLD! I expect that will be a problem anyway, (who doesn't love peeing themselves when they sneeze?) and I don't need any help moving that along.

I wasn't afraid of another C-section, but I did not want the hell of puking again for the first 24-hours of my second child's life. When I met with the anesthesiologist (not the same one as durng my first delivery), she reviewed my chart from Lucas and said, "Why the heck did they give you such a high dose of morphine? No wonder you were puking." *Really? What? Grrr.* She assured me she could regulate my dosages and not cause vomiting, and she was right. I didn't know her name; but for that day, she was my best friend.

After the surgery, I insisted on no narcotic pain meds because again, I didn't want to risk nausea. I can't tell you how many nurses asked me "Are you sure?"

Yes I'm sure! Give me pain over puking any day. Blah. Yuck. And I did fine. Turns out, I had way more other things to think about than my pain.

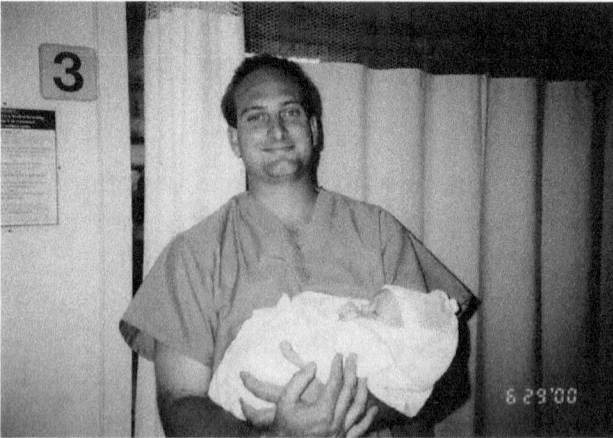

Tony holding Lucas the day he was born.

Chapter Two
Cry Baby

Lucas cried seemingly nonstop from the day he was born until he was 2-and-a-half. But if this is a book about Ben, our second born, then why am I writing about Lucas, our first? Because I truly think everything we learned about parenting, about ourselves, and about each other came from those first few years in testing our patience with an adorable baby (Lucas), who could not seem to be soothed.

What I have learned about Tony through the parenting process is that he can stick with something long after other people get bored and move on. This used to annoy me before children because it meant he could literally watch the same movie three times in a row and not care. *Back to the Future* or *Indiana Jones* or *Twister* would come on TV, and I'd whine "Again?!" It became a joke with us. And yet the same trait that annoyed me was the one that calmed Lucas when Tony would literally swing him in his arms for an hour straight or walk him in the stroller back and forth and back and forth in the house, on our sidewalk, across the street and back, until our fussy boy finally fell asleep.

What I learned about myself was that I was not a very good parent at 3:00 am, and I do better with words than nonverbals. But I quickly learned to breathe and go with the flow and change it up if something didn't work. When I say "not a good parent at 3:00 am," I don't want you to think I was throwing my kid around in frustration. It's just that instead of being patient, exhausted at 3:00 am meant crying with the baby and begging him to talk and tell you what is wrong, please! I suspect other parents have been there…well, probably most parents.

One day soon after Lucas was born, my incision was infected, and I had to go back to the doctor. So Lucas and I went to get my prescription; but before we left the grocery store, he was crying uncontrollably. In the checkout line, people helped me put my groceries on the conveyor, bag them, and take them to the car. They were either super nice to a new mom or were very ready to have that screaming baby out of their store! Another day, my mom came over to help, and Lucas and I were both sobbing in the living room. "What in the world is going on?" she asked. I had no idea what I was doing. As I have often said since then, being a parent is the most rewarding and the most powerless feeling ever.

"Babies cry," they say. "It's just gas," they say.
Uh huh, no. This was not normal. EVENTUALLY, we got an upper g.i. for him, and low and behold, it was obvious he had reflux. (By the way, did you know babies get yummy flavored barium? Why don't they give adults that stuff instead of the white chalk?) Liquid Zantac became a life saver. Thank you, thank you, thank you. Did it stop all of the crying? No, it didn't. But it helped a lot to restore my sanity and give us the breathing room to figure out the rest.

He was still a fussy guy and hard to figure out. Tony's mom had raised four kids of her own and babysat many others; so when it came to comfort level with babies, she was a pro. And yet, she'd have to call me at work to come get Lucas in the middle of the day. "I just can't get him to stop crying. Nothing works." Sometimes the stroller helped or the swing or the car — movement. Sleeping was not his favorite; and for almost a year, he slept in the car seat because that seemed the only thing that comforted him, the closeness of the space. Well that, and Elmo at 3:00 am.

My job is a counselor in private practice. Hence the comment above that communicating with words, easy-peasy. But communication without words — while it is something I definitely use daily — understanding a baby takes some practice. A huge help came from a colleague, a social worker named Susan Baker, who asked me one day if I had ever considered Sensory Processing Disorder. Nope, never heard of it. But finding out about that was another life-altering transition. Not the Big life altering diagnosis, but definitely something that opened our eyes to information that improved all of our lives.

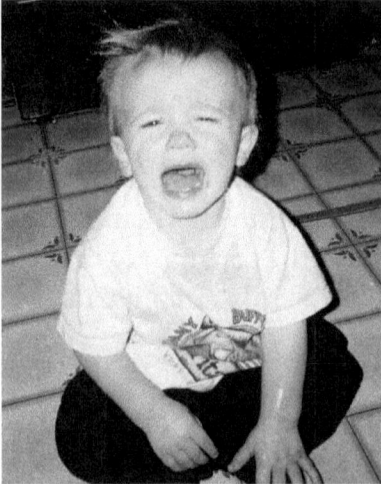

Lucas at age 2, crying. Again.

Chapter Three
It Makes Sense

One time when Lucas was five, I called the pediatrician to ask about a hearing test for him because when I talked to him, he didn't seem to hear. He heard me chatting with the doctor and said, "Mom, I hear fine. I just sometimes don't know which things to listen to." On a general hearing test, he would pass; but where most of us can filter out background noises, people with sensory issues sometimes cannot. Because of this they get overwhelmed and over-stimulated.

In third grade, his teacher said to the class, "We can't go to the library today because of kindergarten screening." Lucas asked, "The kindergartners are screaming?"
This is an example of how the sense of *sound* can be misprocessed. For some people, this is due to sensory issues, like Lucas (and Tony too, we later learned); but for others, it is an auditory processing issue called Central Auditory Processing Disorder or CAPD.

Kids with CAPD often look like they have Attention Deficit Disorder because they don't pay attention in class. But while ADD is often caused by a Dopamine imbalance in the brain, CAPD is a neurological condition that affects how sound is processed and filtered. People with auditory processing issues can get distracted when there are noises, can be over-stimulated in certain acoustics, and can have issues with reading, spelling and vocabulary. If you suspect someone you care about has this, it is tested by an audiologist (talk to an ENT doctor or a hearing/ audiology specialist) and is treated by a speech/ language pathologist. CAPD is not what Lucas had, he had general sensory issues, but it affected his auditory sense also.

Susan Baker set us up for an Occupational Therapy (OT) evaluation through the Missouri First Steps Program when Lucas was two. First Steps is/was (funding continues to get cut) a government funded, early childhood intervention program for children ages 0 to3 to address medical, psychological and behavioral diagnoses. Through this evaluation, we learned that Lucas did have Sensory Processing issues and qualified for weekly OT services that came to the home and the daycare. At this point, Lucas had started in Miss Donna's daycare room at Wee Care, in my opinion the best preschool in the universe. So not only did the OT Gina work with us at home, she also worked with his teachers at school. We were a team, the same team that would later reunite to work with Ben.

Here is the lecture I now give parents in my office about SPD. All of the information we get from the world comes in through our senses. We see, hear, taste, smell, touch it. Then I knock on the table, and say, "When I knock on this table, a message from my knuckles goes through my nerves to my spine to my brain that says, 'That is hard and that is cold and stop doing that,' so I stop knocking." I continue to tell parents that in the same way, information comes in through our senses to communicate with our brain. But in people with SPD, sometimes that information is misinterpreted. For example, one young girl I counseled felt pain whenever she touched paper although she had never told anyone. Schoolwork was torture for her.

Some common things people with sensory issues have trouble with are: tags in clothes, certain fabrics, bare feet on grass, seams on socks or certain shoes. They can have a hard time sleeping or may only sleep with another person and not alone. Plus they can be very picky with foods, only eat certain foods or gag at others, or they don't like noises. The list goes on and on.

Once Lucas was finished with baby food, he would only eat specific foods. It was like his taste buds were exaggerated. The foods he ate (and if you have a kiddo with SPD, this will sound familiar) all seemed to be yellow, white or tan: chicken nuggets, cheese pizza, pizza rolls, milk, cheese sandwich, chips, fries, hot dogs, crackers, peanut butter, Spaghetti-o's, vanilla ice cream. The doctor said, "He'll eat eventually." Nope. He'd rather starve. And gag. No fruit, no veggies, no condiments, no soda — nothing chewy, gooey or mealy — and nothing watery. (He once told me he didn't like things that turned into water in his mouth. I asked him for an example, and he said lettuce. I had never realized it did.) The worst were applesauce and mashed potatoes because he could feel the separate grains in them (exaggerated taste buds!). When he was four, his teacher Miss Diane insisted she could get him to eat applesauce. She offered him a shiny new quarter and he tried, but gagged. So she gave him peanut butter crackers, again, and finally believed me.

When he got older, (around age 6) more educated about SPD and aware, we put a poster board up. Each time he tried a new food, we wrote it on the board, and he put a smile or a frown next to the food. This helped give him credit for trying new things and have self-awareness about the kinds of foods he was eating. Today, at 14, he is still a picky eater(we need to buy stock in Totino's pizza rolls and get our own milk cow!), but he often willingly tries new foods without being asked and recently asked for a multi-vitamin. Go Lucas! I'm glad we didn't force him. As a counselor I worry he would eventually have created an issue with food.

Education is the key. You would think that with all of this junk food, he would not grow or be malnourished and overweight. But he is a giant, (6 foot 1) and he is healthy and trim and smart, smart, smart. We get criticism from people who think we have "given in" to him regarding food, but again, learning to shrug off the criticism helped us later in parenting Ben.

The other things that helped Lucas were through the "sensory diet" Miss Gina taught us to do with him. By diet I don't mean organic foods and gluten free, although I know some people find those helpful. The "sensory diet" was a routine of activities and exercise we did with Lucas multiple times a day to integrate his senses and lesson his anxiety. It worked. An excellent book that educated us is called *The Out of Sync Child* by Carol Stock Kranowitz. If I pull the book off our shelf now, it is marked and highlighted by Tony, who in reading about Lucas, found himself saying, "That's me, that's me."

Things that had always seemed like quirks for Tony finally had a name, like when Tony lost his appetite in noisy restaurants, or he wouldn't be able to "see" things that were tucked away. He was really smart, but a slow reader because of the extra time it took to process the words on a page. It was an ah-ha moment for us as parents working with Lucas, but also for Tony and for me. I've been able to help hundreds of parents and kids since then in my work.

The sensory diet helped to eliminate Lucas's constant crying. We installed a net swing in our basement that he used daily to self-calm. He spun on a sit 'n' spin at preschool daily when he seemed agitated. We had a nylon brush that we used on his arms and an exercise ball we stretched him over. He was "sensory-seeking," so he used a mini trampoline at home, and also benefitted from bear hugs. Sometimes, he buried himself in what Tony called a Lukie-nest, covering himself with blankets and stuffed animals and pillows to sit and watch TV. He was 7 before he finally slept alone, but I was just grateful he was finally sleeping through the night without crying!

It didn't take long at all before these activities became part of our daily life. Initially, it affected his coordination in PE in kindergarten; but now, years later, it's not even something we put on a medical form because it no longer affects his daily life in ways he cannot self-modulate. This year it reared its ugly head when Lucas played JV basketball and had to find a way to fine tune the noises of bouncing balls and squeaky shoes and yelling coaches. But he did it and won most-improved player of the year. The information we learned from Susan and Gina through the First Steps program was invaluable and changed our lives for the better. So when we REALLY had a life-altering event, we knew just who to call.

The pressure of standing on his head was part of Lucas' sensory diet.

Lucas and Ben surrounded by stuffed animals in a Lukie-nest.

Chapter Four
Roller Coaster Ride

Getting pregnant again was a touchy subject. Tony has three sisters and I have one brother, and we are very close to our families. I was adamant that Lucas not be an only child, but Tony was scared out of his mind with all of the issues last time, and he did not want to do that again. But, it happened anyway. I'm not the kind of girl to get pregnant sneakily, but I am sure I probably begged and pleaded until he gave in. During the summer of 2003, we got pregnant. We also decided to refinance our house at a great rate for a short term, and started building one of those wooden play-sets in our yard for Lucas.

We live in a neighborhood in the country that has many houses, but each lot has five acres. So we have the benefit of both great neighbors and privacy. One Sunday that summer, a neighbor was moving and had an open house; and since we had never seen the inside of their house, we decided to go look. It was a beautiful custom home thirty years newer than ours, with more bedrooms, a wood burning stove and hard wood everywhere. As we walked through, I said, "Um, I could live here." And Tony said, "I could live here." And that was that. Sold the house, moved the playset... had a miscarriage. Not the plan.

A "blighted ovum" means the egg and sperm meet but never develop, but the body thinks it's pregnant. So the symptoms are there, and the test is positive. Four weeks in, I felt weird, and two weeks later an ultrasound confirmed no baby. It is something I now know that half or more of all women experience. When you go through it you feel like you are the only one and yet you're not. But it's like a little secret you carry around and don't really talk about. I had a D&C, we settled into our house, and were just fine to find out a month later, we were pregnant again.

Other than the crazy 30-something hour birth, my pregnancy with Lucas had been better than fine. I felt healthier, ate healthier, had less acne, no nausea, loved being pregnant. So I looked forward to doing it again. As anyone who's had a miscarriage knows, the first trimester was nerve-wracking. Wondering, worrying, watching. Biologically, things were going just fine. Environmentally, not so much. New house, (new mortgage), new baby on the way, planned trip to Disney World...and then Tony lost his job. Holy cow. Another curve ball.

If you know Tony Merz, you know he frets about money on his richest day and takes his role as family caretaker very seriously. THIS threw him for a tail spin. Luckily, he has always done side work as a landscaper, even paid his way through college, twice, from the hard work he does. And this is how we stayed afloat until he found his next "real" job. Of course I was working also; but as many people know, one salary barely cuts it these days. Six weeks of scary, and we could relax once again, for a minute.

During pregnancy, there are many, many blood tests. I suspect the desensitization to needles during this time might be intended to prepare mothers for the invasiveness of every employee of the hospital being all up in your girl business during birth, but I'm not so sure. Some are mandatory, and some are not. One optional test at that time was called a Triple Screen Test. It was a "screening" for birth defects like Spina Bifida, Down Syndrome, and others. If the test comes back negative, nothing to worry about. Positive, you go for more tests. Two of my screenings came back negative (no Down Syndrome); but the one screening for possible Spina Bifida was positive, and I was scheduled for a 3-D ultrasound for a closer look.

My college roommate has a daughter with Spina Bifida, and I remember chatting with her during her pregnancy when she found out. Many people opt not to have the Triple Screen Test because they say they'd have the baby regardless of the results, so why does it matter? But in her case, knowing in advance made her doctor decide to have her deliver at a hospital that specializes in this area; and the minute she gave birth, her daughter went into surgery to repair her exposed spine and prepare her the best way possible for the journey ahead. Because of this, I didn't regret having the test; but she was the first friend I called because she knew the panic and fear of getting a test result like this. So many questions, and the imagination takes over, and it isn't pretty what your mind worries about.

In the time, between the screening result and the ultrasound, I talked to many friends and family members. One conversation stands out to me after all of these years because of the irony. We were discussing the possible pending test results; and this friend, being a nurse, stated something to the effect of, "If I had a child with Down Syndrome, I would get an abortion. These kids have so many severe health issues, and their quality of life is not good. I just wouldn't want to do this to a child." At the time, I, a counselor of many kiddos with behavior issues, responded by saying, "Give me health issues over behavior issues any day!"

Now please do not criticize my friend for her comments because she was being sincere and concerned, and actually carries the philosophy of 90 percent of people who are pregnant with Down Syndrome children. The majority end in pregnancy termination, and kids who are born with DS do have significantly more health issues than other kiddos. Now when she sees Ben, she is nothing but accepting and loving, and I'm sure has no recollection of ever making that statement. But it was a statement that I have heard many times in the media ever since and have never forgotten. (On a side note, feel free to criticize me for my statement about having a kiddo with behavior issues because it wasn't a nice thing to say; and now I know even better that when my kid acts out, there is so much more to the story.)

The 3D ultrasound I had to look for Spina Bifida was amazing. I had never seen anything like it. I suspect these days, technology makes ultrasounds look like photographs; but back in the ancient days of 2004, this 3D picture of a real live human being inside of me, where I could actually see the baby's features, was remarkable. The specialist showed me on the screen very clearly what he was looking for and pointed out that there was no sign of exposed spine. All spine and brain looked good, nothing to worry about. He said that if I wanted a more definitive answer, I could have amniocentesis—but a super long needle and more risks to baby? No thanks. His word was good enough for me. Again, ironically, if I had had the test, we would have known Ben had DS.

There was one more event during my pregnancy that was rough at the time, but I had no idea how much the experience would mean to me later. It was the loss and funeral of my friend's nine-year-old son to cancer. The courage of families to deal with childhood cancer is divine. The strength and patience can only come from above because there is nothing more difficult than losing a child. As if it wasn't hard enough to be at the funeral of a child, my hormones and life inside of me had me sobbing uncontrollably, and I was glad to be sitting in the back of the very packed church. When the priest described the strength and faith of my friend as she bathed her son's lifeless body in the hospital after he passed, just as the women had bathed Jesus, I was in awe of the depth of her courage. This image has stayed with me. When we learned months later that Ben had Down Syndrome, I often thought about her son, born healthy with no diagnosis. I realized that even if my child was born healthy, with no diagnosis, that didn't guarantee me a life of no heartache. Nothing can be taken for granted, and knowing from day one (or three) of his life that we had this diagnosis actually gave us better preparation for the years to come.

Chapter Five
Birthday

So other than the dumb decision to go to an outdoor Tim McGraw concert in July in 95 degree heat when I was 9 months pregnant, the rest of my pregnancy was uneventful. (Note to any pregnant women: outdoor summer concerts are not enjoyable in the late stages of pregnancy when you have to stand the whole time surrounded by crazy teenagers who don't let you hear the concert anyway.) It was hot, uncomfortable, and I couldn't wait for it to be over. Luckily this was the worst of being pregnant.

My super close friend of 35 years, Kelly, was pregnant also, and we were due within days of each other. Her baby girl was due soon but was breech, so her doctor had the great idea to manually move the baby around the right direction. That means he climbed up on her belly and pushed and shoved until Riley was head down. OW! Well, you can imagine what happened next, hello Riley! She was like, fine, then here I come! And she was born a week before my planned C-section. We had shared many moments during pregnancy but I was anxious not to share this one.

The day of Ben's birth went great. Lucas went to hang out with Grandma and Grandpa; Tony and I went to our fancy hospital room (have you seen maternity wards these days??), and the anesthesiologist set my mind at ease about puking, so we were ready, right? We went to the operating delivery room, everyone was calm, things were routine, C-section went well, no issues like last time. Then, THEN, life changed forever. For real this time.

Ben was blue, not breathing. There was a flurry in the room as my doctor focused on putting me back together, sewing me up, but the staff pediatrician and nurses frantically went to work on Ben. They got him on oxygen and took him into another room, taking Tony with them. At first I saw my baby across the room being weighed, and I remember thinking his hand looked funny, but I didn't know why. Later Tony came in to see me, and he was very solemn and tearful. He said, "Ben's lungs aren't working on their own. He is on oxygen, and they think he has a disorder."

They actually did DNA testing to determine if he had the extra 21st chromosome of "Trisomy 21", or Down Syndrome; but it takes three days to get the results. During those three days, we were all over the place. He has it; he doesn't have it. My obstetrician and her partner both told me they had often seen false positives on the Triple Screen, but had never seen a false negative. "It just doesn't happen." Ok, whatever, it just did. But because of this, even the OB kept thinking the DNA test would be negative. Children and adults with DS share many physical features that make it obvious they have the extra chromosome, but babies are not so obvious to lay people, in my opinion. Hospital neonatal staff, however, they know. And yet they showed eternal patience with us, as we repeatedly questioned if they were sure.

Eighteen days Ben was in the ICU. For the first three days, I was in the hospital, too, because of the C-section; so I was allowed to go down to ICU and hold my baby any time, day or night. They know what babies and mommas need! That was a blessing.

The other thing I thought I needed was internet to research this syndrome and prepare myself. Yes and no. The amount of information out there is breathtaking, and that's good — because this is a topic that a lot is known about. On the other hand, not all of the information applies to all of the children with DS. For example, a large number of the kiddos have heart defects, but Ben did not. (We are very lucky in that aspect.) So it was overwhelming. I'd read about what he could have or what he could be more prone to, and that would give me a new thing to worry about. On the one hand it was good to be prepared, but sometimes more info can be too much info.

The ICU itself was also overwhelming. While at first we were scared of our future and all of this unknown, a few days in ICU, and we were counting our blessings. Ben was the biggest baby in there. Born at a normal, healthy 6 pounds 8 ounces, he looked like a giant next to the premature babies that fit in their daddies' hands. The little girl next to Ben was born with her intestines on the outside of her body. My friend Lisa, a pediatric ICU nurse for years, explained that the intestines were too swollen to fit in her abdomen, so they hung in a bag above her; and each day, a little more were fed into her body. Babies died. Parents cried. And the nurses did their jobs tirelessly. They were medical staff, but they were also counselors and social workers and friends to all of us scared parents who couldn't do it without them

.

During our own three days in the hospital, waiting for the results and visiting Ben in the ICU, Tony and I also had to finally agree on our baby's full name. We had tossed around many names, and Lucas was easier because he shared a middle name with Tony and his dad. But a middle name for Ben was hard to settle on. Then we were sitting in the hospital room, having lunch, and on the TV came *Raiders of the Lost Ark*, and we started giggling.

Here's the story. Remember I said earlier that Tony would watch the same movies over and over and over until I ran screaming from the room? One of those was Indiana Jones (and another was *Star Wars*). When I was pregnant with Lucas, Tony would often say to my belly, "Luke, I am your father," in his best Darth Vader voice.

When we were in Disney World, we saw a live show of Raiders. And now it was on TV. The name Ben we had just liked the sound of, although it's fun that it goes with the Star Wars theme, too(Ben Kenobi). Seeing Indiana Jones in the hospital solidified the deal, the theme. Middle name was Harrison, as in Harrison Ford.

This was one time I hoped gossip would take over. I was not ashamed of our situation, but it became overwhelming to explain what was going on to everyone we knew. So we told some close friends and let them spread the word. We told our parents and let them tell the rest of the family. I called my office secretary and let her tell my staff. It was a lot to handle in a short period of time every day for us in the hospital. I couldn't bear to tell the story over and over and explain it all and handle their questions. Of course everyone was supportive and loving and wanted to do anything for us and we were grateful. But we had a new normal to adjust to and that was the priority.

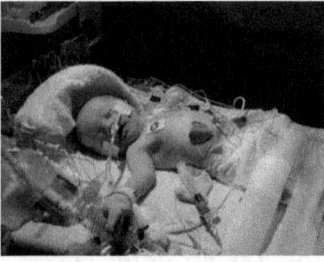

Ben's first day in this world, in the ICU.

Chapter Six
Time Stands Still

Eighteen days in the ICU. Two and a half weeks of time standing still. As anyone who has spent time visiting a hospital day after day knows, our life took on a new routine. Getting Lucas to daycare, driving the hour to the hospital, scrubbing up, spending the day with Baby Ben, meeting with doctors and nurses and therapists to discuss his progress, then going home exhausted to do it all again the next day.
Ben only stayed on the ventilator for 24 hours, but then his lung collapsed, and he needed a chest tube. The first couple of days were rough because of his breathing. At that point, having DS meant nothing because our focus was on keeping him alive. But by the time I was discharged at 72 hours, he was physically doing better. He was moved to a less intense nursery, and we met with a geneticist to get the official DNA results confirming it was definitely Trisomy 21. There was no denying it now.

Because I had a miscarriage before Ben's birth, and because I had had issues birthing Lucas, and because I was 35 , I wondered if I had done something wrong, something to cause this. But the geneticist patiently explained that the genetic factors that determine this happen at the moment of conception. When the sperm meets the egg, the next second the cells start dividing and growing, and an embryo starts forming.   (A DNA map with extra chromosome on 21)

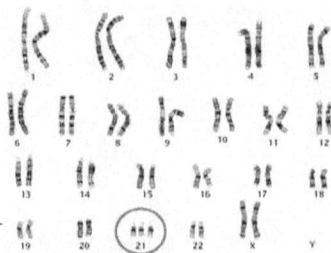

In normal, healthy development, a human has 23 strands of DNA, and each strand has 2 chromosomes, one from each parent for a total of 46 chromosomes. With Down Syndrome, the 21st strand has three chromosomes for some reason, hence the name Trisomy 21. It is this extra on the 21st that causes the issues that are common with most DS people. While becoming pregnant at an older age does increase the risk of any birth defects, there are people who have DS babies when pregnant in their twenties.

There is nothing I could have done to prevent it. There is nothing I did that caused it, and it's not hereditary. So if I had another pregnancy, we have no greater risk of having another child with DS just because we had one. Even with this information, it was difficult for me not to wonder, to doubt myself. It is such a huge responsibility to have a life growing inside of you, is there something I could have done differently to prevent this? Eventually I just had to put that out of my mind, because even if there had been, what's done is done, and we had to focus on Ben getting healthy and released from the hospital.

Even more difficult than visiting my baby in the hospital every day was leaving him there to go home. I knew he was in good hands, and I knew I had another child who needed me also, but the ache on the long hour drive home was excruciating. The nurses said Ben loved attention, and always wanted to be held. He fussed if someone wasn't with him. (Hmmm, foreshadowing? Probably.) That information just made me miss him all the more.

One morning, I arrived at my usual time, and I walked in to find a stranger holding my baby. He was a grandfatherly man, holding him and rocking in a rocking chair. At first, I had the normal response of "Hey who's got my baby!" But then he introduced himself as a hospital volunteer, there to love on the babies, and my heart was filled with relief. To know that my infant son was not alone in a cold bed crying to be held when I wasn't there felt so wonderful. It seemed, again, these ICU people knew exactly what they were doing.

Our mission for those 18 days, once Ben was breathing normally, was to get him to eat from a bottle. Even at this young age, we had a speech therapist and an occupational therapist working with us to find different bottles and nipples that might work, teaching us how to feed him. One common physical characteristic of DS is a larger tongue that protrudes and a higher palette (roof of his mouth). Because of this, his ability to "latch on" to the bottle was limited, and he couldn't be discharged to go home until he could eat from a bottle. In the meantime, he was fed through an NG tube. Each day the nurses measured how much he ate through the tube versus a bottle. It was such a waiting game. Would it be today? Tomorrow? How's he doing, doc? Do you know when it will be? Of course, they had no idea. This was the beginning of us learning that Ben would always do things on his schedule— not ours. Remember how I said having a challenging Baby Lucas prepared us for the patience we needed as future parents? Yeah, the future was now.

Side note: working in the medical field and owning a small business has made me strongly dislike insurance companies. They pay poorly and cost a bazillion dollars. But for once, I got the value of my investment. The day I had my first pregnancy confirmation appointment, I paid a fifteen dollar co-pay. Nine months of pregnancy appointments, C-section birth, three days for me in the hospital and 18 days for Ben, and I never paid another dime. His stay in the ICU alone was $200,000. The insurance company didn't pay the hospital that full amount, but wow, it's no wonder insurance is so expensive. However, in contrast, my obstetrician got paid $75 to do my C-section. A mechanic would get paid more than that to work on my car! Insane.

For years after, driving on the highway past the hospital brought tears to my eyes in remembrance of our days there. The smell of antiseptic soap, visiting people in the hospital, using the hospital issue pacifier, all of these things triggered gut-wrenching memories of our relatively short, but life-changing, visit; and I now have great compassion for any family dealing with long-term hospital stays.

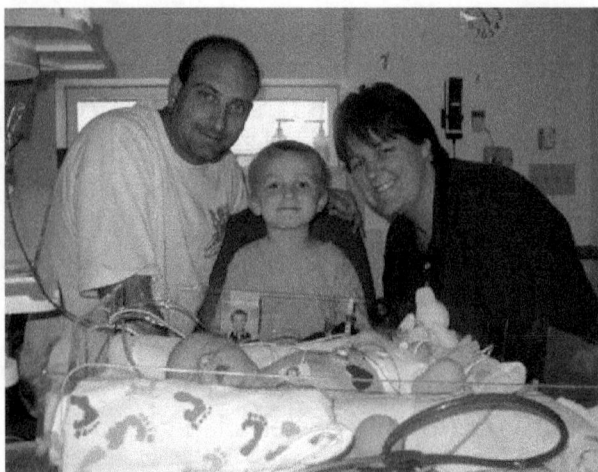

Tony, Lucas and myself with Ben in the ICU.

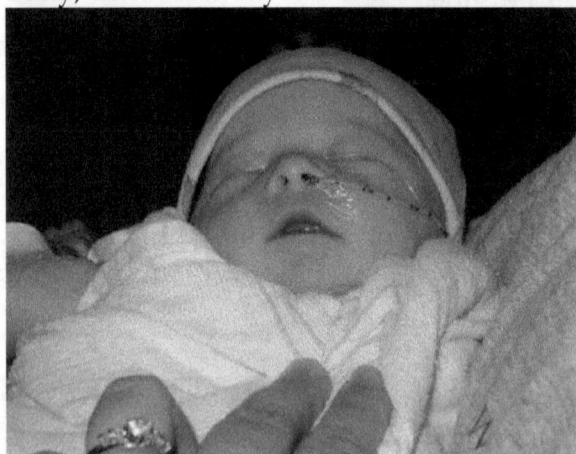

Baby Ben with the NG tube that fed him until he could latch onto a bottle.

Chapter Seven
Ben's Team, Year One

When we learned that Lucas had Sensory Processing issues in 2002, we were lucky to have a social worker named Susan helping us and an Occupational Therapist named Gina seeing him weekly at daycare and at home, teaching us about SPD, and showing us and the daycare staff how to utilize a "sensory diet" with Lucas to help him remain calm. It was these same people I contacted immediately after Ben was born. When someone under the age of 18 has a qualifying medical or behavioral diagnosis, they are eligible for federal and state funded services regardless of income. So while we would likely not qualify for disability funds or Medicaid because of our income, we were able to receive all of the services necessary to help Ben get the best start possible on his development. We absolutely believe this is the reason he has excelled.

From ages 0-3, these services were funded through the Department of Mental Health and from ages 3-5, it was the Early Childhood Special Ed Preschool through our school district. During Ben's first year of life, in one week, we and/or Ben would see seven different team members at home or at daycare, at no cost to us.

Initially, a nurse from Nurses for Newborns saw him weekly to monitor his health. Many children with DS have heart defects, lung issues, hearing deficits, sight impairment, and diminished immune systems. The nurse monitored his health and educated us on what to look for. For example, the Eustacian Tube from his ear to his throat had not fully developed, so he was more prone to ear infections.

A massage therapist saw Ben twice a week because he had torticollis, meaning his head was crooked because of his muscles, caused by the awkward way he sat in the womb. This is common with many babies, not just ones with DS. She taught me how to massage Ben's neck, and also how to massage his abdomen to help with digestion and bowel function. Parents As Teachers saw us in home monthly to assess his developmental milestones.

While in the hospital, we saw a speech therapist, and this continued once we were discharged. In my opinion, this was *the* most important therapy because Ben needed to learn to communicate with people to get his needs met. I have seen first-hand people interact with adults with DS. When some people can't understand what the individual with DS is saying, they ignore him or her. I knew that there would be times in Ben's life when he would be criticized or teased; but if he could learn to communicate, hopefully that would lessen the opportunity for discrimination.

During the first year of his life, the speech therapist didn't work on actual speech, but rather oral health and development. Sucking on a bottle, eating from a spoon, making noises with his mouth, massaging his face to get him aware of his own face — these were his first speech goals. Ben's tongue is not as wide or protruding as some kiddos with DS, but his mouth structure did cause him to eat differently than other babies; and this therapist also helped the daycare staff learn to help Ben.

Another characteristic of DS is what is called hypotonic, or floppy muscle tone. Think of a time when you have held a child and he didn't want you to put him down, so he went limp in your arms. That way, he wouldn't have been able to stand when you put him down. That limpness is what DS kids deal with their whole lives. It is not always obvious, but even as they age their muscles aren't tone and they tire easily. As toddlers it is more difficult for them to stand and walk and hold their own weight. These became the goals of Ben's physical therapist. Exercising his muscles and teaching us to do the same helped us to set realistic developmental goals for him.

I never knew what to expect regarding milestones for Ben. Generally parents know kids will sit up around 6 months and walk at about 12 months. But there isn't a standard expectation for kids with DS because they are all so different and develop at their own rate.

We learned to compare Ben to himself instead. I realized that he would eventually meet the milestones of every other kiddo, but it would take him longer. So instead of crawling for 6 months, he did for 10. And what a funny crawl that was! His funny floppy muscles prevented him from crawling the same way as most kids, and yet he could do things other kids could not. For example, he would sit up, balance on his tailbone, point his arms and legs out straight and make the funniest face ever. Other times he would sit on the kitchen floor and use his foot to turn himself round and round in a circle, over and over. His version of crawling was sitting on his butt, one leg bent in front of him and one leg behind, and he used his hands to launch himself to hop hop hop across the room. He was a creative nut who hopped to the beat of his own drum and still does.

Our pediatrician did not have a lot of experience with DS kids; and if I had wanted to, I could have set Ben up with a clinic at the local children's hospital that specialized in DS. But our doctor did his own extensive research and has been fantastic at setting us up for any and every specialized test suggested. He has stayed on top of Ben's health tremendously. The staff at his office got to know us well since Ben seemed to catch a cold or an ear infection every 6 weeks; but just like everywhere Ben goes, he became a celebrity. While other kids waited patiently with their families in the waiting room, Ben would stroll in (later when he could walk, and still now) to the cheers of "Hey Ben! What's up Ben? High five, Ben!" Because we live in a small community, we have had the convenience of Ben's therapists following him from place to place. We still have the same social worker since the day he was born; and today at age 10, he has the same Occupational Therapist he had from an infant. Gina has helped teach Ben how to eat, to brush his teeth, to tolerate haircuts, to write his name, to button his shirt and zip his jacket. Her expertise, creativity and eternal patience have again enabled Ben to be more independent every day.

With all of these people in and out of Ben's life, unfortunately he comes in contact with many germs; and having DS makes him more prone to weak immunity. This is just a fact of life; and in the long run, being around germs and dirt has probably helped his immune system. That first year, however, somehow, somewhere, he got a rash that was not able to be diagnosed for months. At first, the doctor thought it was eczema and prescribed a cream that only minimally helped. The rash started on his hands and spread to his torso, and eventually covered his whole body. Soon we all had it, including me , Tony, Lucas, even aunts and uncles and grandparents.

Finally I took Ben to a dermatologist who looked and touched and hummed and hawed and finally went to her computer. She came back and said, "No way! I haven't seen this in years! And I've never seen a case this bad." It was SCABIES! Holy cow, what a nightmare.

Scabies are critters like lice or fleas or bedbugs, nearly impossible to get rid of. They burrow under your skin and lay eggs *under your skin* and hatch and grow and—gross! They itch terribly, and they are red bumps. We had to clean and wash everything and use special medicine—it was horrible. The doctor said Ben should have been crying and screaming in misery because his case was so bad; but because he had Down Syndrome and he was so relaxed about everything, he didn't. Poor, poor guy.

One piece of advice we had to follow was to put the stuffed animals and the couch cushions in trash bags for days. Then I would let the bugs die and vacuum them up. My couch cushions were attached to each other and too big to fit in trash bags, so I had the grand idea to pull out all of the stuffing and let it sit in bags for days. Needless to say I ruined the couch, but we finally did get rid of those parasitic creatures.

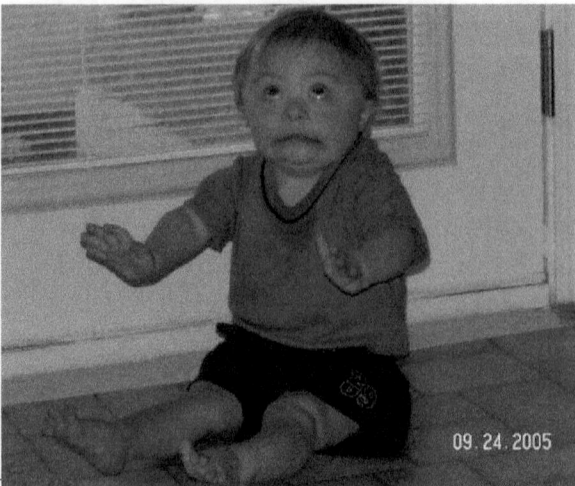

Ben balancing on his tailbone making a goofy face.

09.24.2005

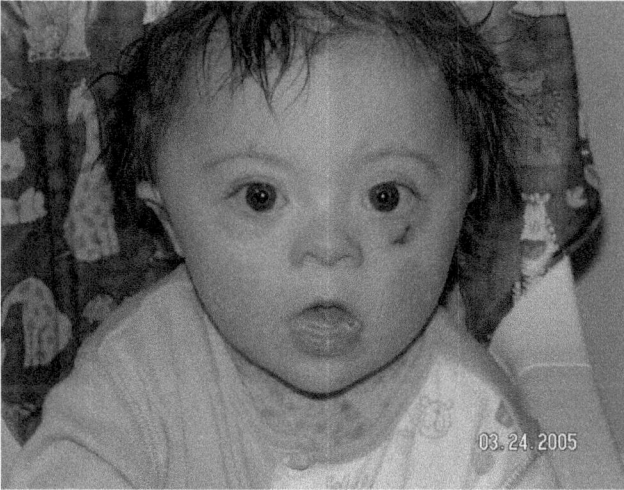

Scabies. Poor, poor Ben.

Chapter Eight
Ben's Aura

Once we got over that bug crisis and settled into a routine, life took on a "new normal" for us. Tony and I worked; the boys went to daycare; therapists saw Ben at daycare; and every couple months, we were at the pediatrician with a sinus or ear infection. Luckily, I am my own boss, so getting off work isn't a problem. There are many stresses of being a small business owner; but making my own schedule is a giant perk, especially with kids.

As I stated earlier, Ben's developmental milestones do not come according to a typical schedule; so each academic advancement has also been a team decision, balancing his cognitive and physical abilities and what is in his best interest. When we discussed moving him from the infant room to the toddler room at daycare, he was not yet walking. His peers were age 1 to 2 years; and though toddling all around, they weren't exactly steady on their feet. I didn't expect they would hurt Ben; but because he could only still crawl, I worried they would trip over him or bump into him, and he wouldn't be able to defend himself. Ha, boy was I wrong!

I learned that year, and every year since, that Ben is no chump. If there is an altercation among kids, he was probably the aggressor. I don't mean to say he's *aggressive*, but he also isn't a pushover. As a matter of fact, somehow he seems to have an aura about him that people sense and respond to. Many people respond favorably to folks with DS. People assume that they are kind and happy and loving, which is not necessarily always the case. Don't get me wrong, Ben can turn on the charm. But he also has his share of grumpy days.

But this aura of Ben's was something more. It is unspeakable. People, children, strangers are drawn to him. In that one-year-old class, where he sat on the floor surrounded by toddlers, the kids took care of him. They nurtured him. They protected him. My worries were in vain and should probably have been for the other kids because Ben was the one who tried to push them around. I am sure this was his way of communicating because he was not yet talking. But this same energy has followed him since. People know Ben everywhere he goes, as if he is a celebrity.

When he was three or four, his Developmental Therapist had a talk with his teachers, informing them not to be afraid to push him, to expect more from him. Don't dress him; don't feed him. Let him try to do it himself first. Ben has always been smarter than he's given credit for—more clever, too; and if someone will do something for him, he will let them. He'll say, "I'm tired," or "I'm sick," to get out of something he doesn't want to do. Unfortunately for him, we've learned to read him pretty well, and we respond with, "No you're not. Get up and do it." And then he does, after he's sure you're not going to do it for him.

During first grade, I went with him to a birthday party held at an indoor gym. His school friends were there, and everyone was shooting baskets. I watched as Ben tried to make a basket. Each time the ball went flying the other way, a different kid would chase it and bring it back to him and say, "Here ya go, Ben." What? This kid was milking the system! He didn't ask them to get the ball for him when he missed; they just did it. And he certainly didn't complain.

One weekend, we were at our school football game; and as Ben, a third grader, and I walked to the concession stand, every thirty seconds, someone would say, "Hi Ben!" Second graders, fifth graders, high schoolers, "Hi Ben!" And Ben would respond in kind. "Hi Katie. Hi Paul. Hi Cameron. Hi Darren. Hi Grace." He knew them all, and they knew him. At the local drive thru window, the worker said, "Where's Ben today?" Leaving school one day, a man, who I think is either a janitor or a bus driver, said "What's up, Ben?" People at restaurants give him extra stuff, the grocery store lady and the Walmart lady always give him stickers. The kid is a celebrity, and he's working it in his favor.

My favorite line to him is, "It's a good thing you're cute, because that's the only thing that saves you sometimes." I have found that even people who have never met Ben are affected by him. I post his stories on my Facebook page, and people will write to say how much they love to hear about him. My mom will go to the hairdresser, and they will swap stories as the stylist also has a relative with DS. When Ben is happy and smiling, it is huge, and it is contagious. He says "I rock!" and yes, he does.

Not everyone is a big fan of The Ben however. While some people are drawn to him, I notice that some people shy away. I'm not sure if it is discomfort or ignorance or discrimination; but while some people are so patient with him and anxious to see what he's going to do next, others seem intimidated by the thought of him.

One incident hurt my feelings, although luckily he was unaware. We were at a gathering with many adults and kids, and the kids asked if they could have a sleepover together. I heard the parent tell their child, "Well, all but Ben, because I don't know how to take care of him." At this age, Ben was probably five and didn't require much more "care" than any other kid for a sleepover, but I suppose the parent didn't know that. I could have let Lucas spend the night without Ben, but I didn't. I explained the reason why, and Lucas understood. If I try to tell Ben why he can't do something the other kids are doing, that doesn't go over well. He believes he is just like every other kid. People ask me if Ben knows he has a diagnosis, and I don't think so. He's just Ben. And the world kind of revolves around him.

To clarify, in spite of being the center of attention everywhere he goes, Ben is not selfish—quite the opposite. His empathy is off the charts. Even before he could communicate with words, he could sense energy and feeling. He is sad when others are sad and happy when they are. He cries when SpongeBob cries (which is almost every episode—SpongeBob is a crybaby!), and gets mad when Squidward is mean, "Not nice, Mom!" If he gets himself a juice box from the fridge, he will get one for his brother, too, even if Lucas didn't ask for one. When you arrive at our house, he opens the door wide, says "Come in!" and announces to everyone near that you have arrived: "Here's Mommy!" It feels pretty good to be presented like royalty. When I recently had the flu, he made a large glass of ice water and brought it to me to help me get better. He'll make up a song for people on his guitar or his harmonica, and it will be rockin' for the men and slow and sweet for the ladies. He gets it. And he's a charmer.

He is a unique individual. Having the extra chromosome causes many similarities in people with DS. And yet, just like anyone, he has his own personality that he is well known for. From day one, he has moaned and "talked" in his sleep, and sucked on his tongue to soothe himself. He is social and doesn't like to sleep because he doesn't want to miss anything. For years, he has slept on the couch to be near everyone, even falling asleep sitting up half the time—stubborn. But if he has a bad dream in the night or doesn't feel good, he is impossible to wake up.

He's a mimic, and he loves to make people laugh, even re-enacting inappropriate things like a booty shake or finding the one bad word in a song just to get a reaction from someone. We know darn well that if we laugh at something inappropriate he says, our praise just reinforces it. And yet sometimes, it is so hard not to. One day, we were sitting on the neighbor's porch and a car drove by, and he blurted, "What the hell was *that*?" We were tortured trying to hold in our giggles, and he knew it because he was grinning from ear to ear.

Other things he says sound so unique coming from him, and yet later we realize he learned the words from us. He'll say, "Huh, good point," and later I will hear myself saying that to a client. Did he learn it from me or did I learn it from him? Many people say, "Oh snap!" But hearing it come from Ben, used at exactly the right moment, can really get us laughing. His timing is spot on.

He loves to admire himself in the mirror, and our friend Ginny who is a hair stylist insists this is part of the reason why he had meltdowns during haircuts for years. Part of it was because of his history of ear infections and tubes and sensitivity, but the other part was him watching himself have a fit in the mirror, knowing we were watching too, and begging him to relax and survive the haircut. You should have seen our antics. We would delay the cut as long as possible, until he looked less like Justin Bieber and more like the shaggy dog, because we knew he'd have a fit. Then Ginny and I would distract him with singing and dancing and videos and goofiness, all while she tried to cut his locks without chopping off an ear. It wasn't until age nine that he finally relaxed and allowed the cut. And most likely because he has gotten our attention some other way.

He acts according to our reactions; but he also acts like the people he loves, especially his big brother. Anything Lucas and his friend Mitchell do, Ben wants to do. Playing video games, using a computer, hanging with the guys, he wants it all. He uses our words right back at us, such as, "Five minutes. K, Mom?" At a restaurant, he will walk from table to table, pretending to be a waiter taking orders. One day, he walked up to a man in a cowboy hat and said, "Hey there, Cowboy!" We were so embarrassed, but it's one of our favorite stories to tell.

He picks up on patterns, too, that we don't realize are there — like how people in a group will take turns talking and telling stories. One day, he stopped the whole group of people we were having lunch with and said, "Wait, wait! Ben's turn." He got up and stood behind his chair and told a long animated story to everyone. When he was done, he sat down, looked at the person next to him and said, "Your turn."

The other thing we love about Ben is his unique way of saying things. He will use an original Ben-phrase for a while and then eventually use a more correct one, but the rest of us keep using Ben-language. "What say you?" and "I fine" and "Aw, fluffy bug!" are just a few. Uncle Scott and Aunt Suzie serve "shausage" for breakfast; we all say, "Goood day!"

At Thanksgiving this year, we tried to get him to try something new, telling him it was delicious. He responded by saying, "I hate delicious!" and now one of us says that daily. We will drive over the river bridge and say, "There's the 'ribber', Ben," and he will now correct us by saying river. As well he should because he gets smarter every day. We don't do these things to poke fun at him. If you could hear these phrases come from him, you would agree they are cute and funny and so typical of our funny man, Ben.

Rockin Out.

Chapter Nine
Health and Development

When Ben was born, I was given the phone number and website of the Down Syndrome Association of St. Louis, DGASL. They are an amazing resource for new parents, but also throughout the lifespan of a child. They have a lending library and support groups; they raise funds for research and provide excellent social opportunities. Since then, I have found many other resources worldwide, but this local one was a beacon of light when we first got the diagnosis.
They gave us a book titled *Babies With Down Syndrome* by Karen Stray-Gunderson. This was an excellent first resource of what to expect. We also received from somewhere a DVD about what to expect the first years. At the time, I wanted to suck up as much information as I could. Being a new parent is powerless enough without the unending questions of a diagnosis we'd never dealt with before.

In the literature, we learned there are many common health issues that people with DS are more prone to. These include hearing loss, ear infections, poor vision, thyroid disorder, c-spine weakness, heart defects, slow lung development, low IQ, delayed development, intestinal and digestive issues, behavioral issues, ADHD, autism, leukemia, very early onset Alzheimer's, and shortened life span, to name a few. That was a lot to take in.

At birth, Ben had difficulty breathing and was on oxygen; but once this was resolved, we have not had any major lung issues. Over the years, he would wheeze when he got a cold, and we used Albuteral with a nebulizer; But now I don't even list asthma on a medical sheet because we haven't seen it in years.

For the first few years of his life, we were frequent fliers at the doctor's office. It was mostly ear infections and strep because his Eustachian tubes had not fully developed, so fluid built up instead of draining. At age 2, he got tubes; and at 4, he got tubes and his adenoids taken out, Finally, at age 5 he had his tonsils taken out. At least I think that was the age and order — it's all a blur looking back. Since removing his tonsils, his immune system has really improved. Thank you, Dr. Stroble, ENT! We do still occasionally have ear issues and upper respiratory stuff, but no more than any other family. And by the way, tubes make for a much more enjoyable airplane ride with a baby, just sayin'.

We have luckily never had any heart or lung issues. He was tested for allergies and has some seasonal stuff, but I think that is more hereditary from Tony's side than from DS. Using so many antibiotics during those first five years caused some build up and hive reactions, but we were able to find others to do the trick. Repeated ear infections have affected his hearing at some frequencies, but not enough to need intervention. I do wonder if the ear issues affect his head sensitivity, though, because for years, he hated his hair washed or touched or brushed. Regarding vision, so far so good, but we're keeping an eye on it, of course.

I think removing his tonsils also helped him sleep. He still doesn't like to sleep, but now it's because he doesn't want to miss anything. Before the tonsillectomy, he would sleep with his butt in the air and kick and moan and groan all night. Turns out, these can be signs of obstructive sleep apnea in kids, and I think getting rid of the tonsils removed that blockage. We also see an endocrinologist, although I'm currently in the process of finding a new one because the one we have is just kind of weird. We insist we can tell if Ben has missed his thyroid meds for more than a day—he is a bear. She says that there's no correlation, so we just say, "Uh huh, whatever"; and of course, we try not to miss any meds.

At one point, I read a suggestion about creating a binder for Ben. Each section would address a different topic, like meds, specialists, therapists, developmental milestones, important phone numbers, his school IEP. The closest I got was buying the binder and dividers and throwing papers in a box for when I had time to organize them. It's nine years later, when I find the time, I'll let you know. But it seemed like a great idea. In terms of development, Ben has always marched to the beat of his own drum. He has met all of the milestones babies and kids meet, just later than expected. He crawled that funny crawl until he was 18 months, and then finally walked. Later his PT taught him to climb stairs by starting with a 2-inch block off the ground. Later, she taught him to go up steps foot after foot, instead of one foot at a time. It was interesting to see what she noticed that we did not. She also recommended corrective shoe inserts because his feet turned in slightly. He hated them, but they helped.

He has never been a picky eater, although he certainly has his favorite foods. If you ever meet him, he will tell you his favorites immediately and ask if you want to go out to dinner. At times, he is a bottomless pit, and we have to cut him off. And yet, he doesn't like candy or soda or many things generally bad for him. He'd just as soon eat a can of beans or peas as a bar of chocolate. But he'll eat the whole can.

While potty training went pretty well with Ben, thanks to the daycare's help, his bowels have always seemed to be those of an adult man's, probably because of his voracious appetite. He is easily constipated; and actually, he would only poop in the bath tub until he was 7. That was a fun experience — Tony and I trading daily poop duties. "Your turn!" And if there was a poop explosion, all bets were off. Since turning 9, he has made great progress in the poop department — most likely due to the praise and attention given daily for a "good poop! Nice one!" Interestingly enough, though, he doesn't have accidents. As a matter of fact, he will go all day without peeing if you don't remind him. He does not seem to have the urge to go. We no longer ask if he has to go; we just say go. At 9, he still wore pull-ups at night, and Tony kept asking me when Ben would outgrow them. My answer is that he won't until he senses the urge to pee during the day when he is awake. Kind of strange, but I think it is a sensory thing. An OT explained that one thing that contributes to the constipation is that the muscle needed to push out the poop is also a floppy muscle, so it doesn't feel the urge until the stool is hard and heavy. Now it makes sense why he has grown man poop.

Speech development is my priority for him because as I stated, he must be able to communicate his needs. If he is lost or alone, if he has a job someday, or if he just simply wants to have friends, it is so important that he be able to share his thoughts effectively. He learned receptive language first, but expressive language has been more difficult—probably due to the mechanics of his ears and mouth structure. For example, in receptive language, he could understand what we were saying and what we wanted him to do. "Go in your room, get your shoes, and bring them here." This is a three-step command that he could do sooner than expected. But if you ask him a question and expect an answer, he may not be able to give it, or you may not understand what he is saying.

Just last week a neighbor asked me politely, "Should I be able to understand everything your son is saying?" Can he? Obviously not. Should he? Probably not. Should he try as much as he can? I hope so. My answer was to give him clues to understanding Ben. Try to look at the context of what he is saying, and you will get clues. Also, when he is very excited, and he has a long, fast story, no one can really understand him. The neighbor asked if Ben gets mad when we don't understand him. Oh yes, he most certainly does.
Initially, I thought these questions were a bit rude; but in retrospect I am glad we had the conversation because at least this person was being honest and asking for help communicating with Ben. I am glad he cared enough to ask and not just ignore Ben because that is my fear. Although I'm not sure Ben will ever let anyone ignore him. He enjoys being the center of attention too much.

Recent observations note that he seems to have a delay processing information. If you give him a command, he may not immediately respond; but if you say nothing for 30 seconds, he will usually get up and do it. He also insists that when he is talking to you, you must repeat his words back to him. I think this is his way of assuring you understand what he is saying. Heck, maybe that is why he is always repeating what we say. One thing is for sure, when he is on a roll, he will talk and talk and talk, and you better pay attention or he will notice.

Academically, intellectually, this kid seems to find his own way of doing things. Because his fingers and especially his thumbs are shorter than most, he found his own way to hold a pencil. He struggles to read and write, and yet he can scroll through the guide on the TV and find a show he likes by name. He can work a mouse on a computer and find the software he wants. He can turn things on he wants to play with. He can unlock doors and buckle (and unbuckle) his own seatbelt. He doesn't like putting on his own socks, but he can throw on his crocs in two seconds flat. On my iPhone, he can find the exact song he wants on the album he wants, according to his mood, and then sing every word.

When he was transferring from early childhood to kindergarten, they had to do an IQ test to update his IEP. This was a nonverbal test instead of the traditional one, and was also hindered because he had a broken arm in a cast (from the trampoline, which he still loves). And yet, while we expected his IQ to be low due to the DS, he scored at an 89, which is average for any person. *This normal score* presented a dilemma.

To qualify for special ed, he needed to have a certain amount or delay, and this IQ test did not indicate that. None of us on the team felt if he did a traditional verbal IQ test, he would score that high; he didn't have the verbal skills. But this taught me something about Ben. On a standardized test, he will not score equal to his peers. But he is no dummy. This kiddo has the gift of ingenuity. When he has a mission, he will find a way. We had to find another way to qualify him for his IEP, but I also think we are going to have to find another way to teach him what he needs to know because he has strengths we still aren't aware of. I have no doubt he will show us when he is ready.

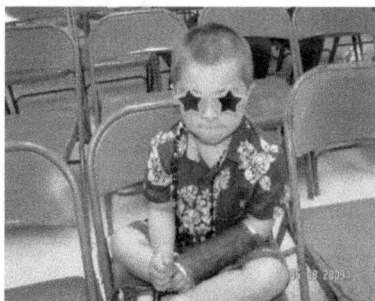

Even with a broken arm he is a star.

Preschool graduation.

Chapter Ten
Put _Me_ In Time Out

This kid wears me out. It literally takes all three of us — me, Tony and Lucas — to get him to behave sometimes, like a tag team. Family, friends teachers say I'm not consistent enough; I give in too easily; I let him get away with things. I like to say, "I choose my battles." And I mean it.

Look, I know what it takes to get results from a child with challenging behaviors; I teach that to parents who come to see me in my practice every day. But no amount of schooling or experience prepared me for Ben and certainly not raising Lucas. Once Lucas got through his sensory issues, he has been a perfect child. Of course I think that, he's my kid and I'm biased; but really, he is sensitive, conscientious, easy going and agreeable. He's responsible and helpful, and he rarely complains. And boy, were we spoiled by him.

Benjamin Harrison Merz is an enigma. Whatever you think should work, do the opposite because that's how things go with Ben.

Yes, he has empathy and can sense emotions in others. But he has no concept of danger. Running through a parking lot, un-phased by a stern talking to or even yelling; deciding to take a walk without telling anyone; locking himself in Grandma's bathroom — no fear. Until about age 8, he did not get the concept of warnings or threats of consequences or counting to three before getting in trouble. Even now, it takes him a bit to process.

Processing is definitely the issue. At times I thought he was ADD, because his mind or his mood could change in an instant. For example, at age 9, he woke up early, was in a good mood, got dressed on time, had fun and laughs in the car on the way to school, dropped off Lucas, chatted about his day, and then when it was time to get out of the car for his school, he said, "No, I stay here." What? What happened? We were doing so well. I have no idea what changed his mind or his mood; but suddenly, he was in stubborn mode and refused to get out of the car.

So here are my tactics. First I tried to joke with him and remind him of the fun we were just discussing. No go. Then I sat quietly because sometimes after a few minutes, he changes his mind. Nope. Then I got out of the car and opened his door and said he had better get out and go into school or he would lose his video game for the afternoon (that worked yesterday). He didn't care. Then I stepped away from the car and pretended to look at my phone for a few minutes while he processed. After a lot of time went by, I shifted gears and changed the subject. "Hey, this Friday, Grandma is coming over!" He responded, "She is? Awesome!" Then he jumped out of the car and jogged into school—just like that.

Every day it is different. Sometimes threat of consequences works, sometimes anticipation of something new or different, sometimes a bribe. The most successful is if one of his favorite people is available to help shift his mood. That would be Lucas or Uncle Scott or Cousin Sam or Daddy. When I'm desperate, I'll call Scott or Tony and have them chat with him on the phone, and that will shift his mood. It's like his brain gets stuck on something; and if I can just shift gears, I can get him back on track. It is exhausting, but it's the only thing we have found that works. At age 10, he got out of the school every morning just fine. It's like he outgrew it. He's still not a morning person, but things keep getting better.

At the risk of jinxing ourselves by saying this, his running away has lessened over the years, but used to be a big concern. Lucas said we needed to get him a shock collar! Of course, we wouldn't, but I did look into a GPS unit. At our house, we have five acres, and so do all of our 20 neighbors — we are surrounded by woods. Many days, Tony and the boys went for a walk down our road and back. So, of course, Ben assumed he could take himself for a walk, right? He'd say, "I'm going to Abby's (a neighbor)," and head for the door. Oh no, you don't! You can't just leave. But he saw no reason not to. He had no idea he wouldn't find his way back.

We have learned at home to touch base with each other. Who's got Ben? Ok, I'm going upstairs, you got him? Otherwise, he'd disappear. One day, he showed up at the house across the street, and they called to say "We've got Ben." Another day, he walked two doors down to play on the neighbor's trampoline (they took it down the next day). One day, he went swimming with the dog in the neighbor's pool — naked! Luckily, she was there. Another day he walked in the woods into a big field next to our house. We were all out looking, on foot, with the neighbor Mike on a four wheeler, me in the car, in every direction. Tony found him five minutes later across a field; but when he called out his name, Ben looked back, saw him and ran. He thought it was a game.
One year at a Six Flags water-park, Ben didn't want to go home. He was probably three. We were drying off, putting on shoes etc, and Ben took off. Imagine me in my swim suit and Tony with one sock chasing Ben through the water park. He was so fast! He ran through the people, behind the scenes, down the sidewalk, until he ended up in an employees' only section and a dead end. We were exhausted and embarrassed. We've never been back.
At my brother's house, he wandered across five yards to play on a neighbor's play set. Well, wandered isn't the correct word because he was on a mission. He usually is. Even if we are walking together, if he sees something he wants, he goes. We have learned to see the world through his eyes. Can he escape? Is something going to trigger him? Should we walk around to avoid something he'd run to?

One day, I watched a friend walking with him along a road at a campground. The friend had him by the hand, but Ben was on the side closest to the road. Before I could even say anything, Lucas walked up and placed himself between Ben and the road. I'm not even sure Lukie realized he did this. This has become our new way of thinking. We have to stay one step ahead of Ben, literally and figuratively.

At home, we raised the garage door opener higher on the wall, so he can't reach. We put extra locks up high on the doors in the house, where he can't reach. We installed door alarms on the doors. We informed all of our neighbors of his tendency to wander.

At school one day, he went from his resource room to his classroom, but the class had gone to recess. Ben thought school was over; so like a smart, young man, he got his book-bag and his jacket and went to the bus. When the bus wasn't where it should be, he went outside and started walking to the high school, where the bus goes next. No dummy, this boy. Luckily, a teacher saw him, and of course she knew Ben. After she said hello, she walked him to the nearest school office, the high school. In the meantime, the elementary was in chaos because no one could find Ben.

At the high school, the principal knew Ben very well because his son and Lucas were best friends, so he chatted with Ben and called the elementary. Whew! They were relieved. They talked to us and apologized and went on and on. We weren't mad. This was par for the course with us and Ben. But it really could have been a disaster if he had gone a different direction. After that, the school purchased a tracking device that looks like a cute fish watch, which Ben wears. If he goes so many yards away from the teacher, her beeper chimes an alert. Now getting him to wear the watch is another story, since two months later, he learned how to take it off. We had to order a different one. After one wander where 911 was called, the emergency personnel said they get hese calls all the time and kids with disabilities tend to wander toward water and woods. Why, I don't know. He said call 911 the second you learn a kiddo has wandered off. Good info.

So overwhelming, at times, I just felt like a bad parent. I couldn't control my child. And other people have always readily given me parenting advice on how to get better results. Just say no. Just stick to it. You give in too easily. I'm a pushover. At this point, that may be so. I'm tired. Some days are better than others, of course, and some are not.

Then one day I signed Ben up for camp with an organization called TASK (Team Activities for Special Kids). Amazing people! They do sports, activities and camps for kids and adults with special needs. On the application, one question caught my eye: "Does your child have an issue with eloping?" Eloping! There was a name for what Ben was doing! Other parents deal with this also? And it is common enough to be on a registration form? Oh, halleluiah, I thought. Not that I'm glad it happens to others, I'm just relieved we are not alone, and these people at the camp aren't freaked out by it. I started to feel less like a bad parent and more like a normal one.

One summer we were signing Lucas up for a summer camp and we discussed signing Ben up also. We knew our daycare could handle him. They knew him, how to think like him, how to get results out of him. But we were concerned that a regular everyday camp would lose him. But when we signed up Ben for a kickball league through TASK, we were elated to see how they handled the kids. Lucas had counted that with 15 kids on the team, there were 27 runaway attempts, and Ben wasn't one of them. And the staff took it in stride. They knew what to expect and how to redirect, and they had more than enough volunteers to take care of it. That summer and the next Ben did two weeks of day camp with TASK, and I have never felt so secure leaving my child with someone. They were amazing. And I wasn't the worst parent on Earth after all.

pouting

spending his birthday at TASK Camp

Chapter Eleven
Functional Dysfunctional Behavior

Ben's behavior can be frustrating and confusing for his family, but in reality probably serves a purpose for him. We just don't always know what it is. For example, one common behavior of his is stopping what he is doing and sitting down *anywhere*, refusing to move. This could be in the middle of crossing the street or in the classroom or in the car when it's time to go. As stated, Ben has always been better at receptive language than expressive language, which means he is better at understanding things we tell him than he is expressing his thoughts and feelings. So he finds other ways to express himself. Because of the hypotonic floppy muscles, he gets physically worn out sooner than other people, so that might be a reason he sits — he's tired. School work may be too hard, or more likely with him too boring, and he doesn't want to keep doing it, so he just stops.

School mornings are rough for us but weekends, no problem. He wakes right up on a Saturday and is ready to party, no matter what time. But on school days, he stays asleep or pretends to sleep, argues or whines or says he is sick or tired. Is this because he is sick or tired? Because he doesn't like the school work or he is bored or it's hard? Is there something or someone he is avoiding at school? I just don't know, and he is not good at putting his feelings into words. So again, we get creative with our tactics, and Lucas is a huge help. We blast music, or we enlist the chaos of the dog to wrestle and lick, or Lucas feigns the need for a superhero to come save him and usually, something gets Ben going. Usually.

Not surprisingly, his behavior also seems to serve the purpose of getting him attention. He loves to be the star. At school this year, he has a new red baseball cap to signify he is the recess line leader. Because he was refusing to come in from playing, his teachers used his desire for attention to get him excited to comply, and it worked. He is very social, loves his friends and enjoys entertaining.

But he also doesn't know when to turn it off, so he gets in trouble for talking in class, farting and giggling, wiggling his booty and getting in the business of the kids in class. I am constantly reprimanding Tony for teaching him silly things, like, "Sorry, sucka!" I said, "If he gets suspended from kindergarten, that's on you, dude." Just like a toddler who picks up his parents' bad habits, Ben mimics the good, the bad and the ugly; and it takes a while to extinguish the bad and the ugly. He very much likes to please people and gets angry and verbally aggressive if he gets in trouble. If reprimanded for even something simple, his response is, "No! Stop it!" If he misbehaves toward someone else, he plays the victim. "They hurt me." No, they didn't, but he doesn't want to get in trouble. He will cry if someone gets mad at him, trying to solicit sympathy. I'm tellin ya, this kid is clever. He has tried repeatedly to fire his teacher, but so far she has won the battle.

Chapter Twelve
Ben's Favorite Things

One thing is certain about Ben, he is unique. He has a list of
favorite things. If you know Ben, you know what he loves —
and you can probably list them. At the top of the list,
maintaining the greatest longevity as a Ben fav, has to be
SpongeBob. We have seen every episode multiple times, have
every CD, every game and a wardrobe full of t-shirts. It is the
video on standby for times of stress, crabbiness or a needed
distraction. He gets very upset when SpongeBob cries and has
also learned about how mean friends can be by watching
Squidward and Plankton. He is definitely a TV kid; and
having various electronic devices has helped us with the
previously described discipline when we need to give him
time to chill or reframe. Scooby Doo, Iron Man, Shrek and
most especially music videos could play on a repeated loop,
and he would be occupied.

His other love from birth has been water. He would take three
baths in a day if we'd let him, play on a water slide no matter
how cold and is a natural swimmer. He could hold his breath
under water at such a young age that at first we freaked out.
But his response was, "Did you see that?" The other day, it
was 45 degrees outside, and Ben put on his swim suit and
asked to get in the pool. He was very angry when I told him
the pool is closed for the winter and has a cover on it. I would
have taken him out there to dip his toe in the cold water to
see, but he would swim naked in a blizzard if we'd let him,
and that's not an exaggeration. Tony has a boat that we use on
the local rivers, and the boys spend hours swimming out
there, catching turtles and tadpoles and playing on the
sandbars.

Ben loves music, and not just any music. For a while he tolerated kid tunes, like Veggie Tales and the Chipmunks, but now he has very specific tastes. He likes pop and rock, hip hop and country, but no slow ballads because he says, "Those are dumb, Mom."

What is especially interesting is that if someone plays or enjoys a song in his company once, he will remember and play it for them again later. For example, he played Taylor Swift for his cousin Allison after hearing her play it months before. He also played a Train song for our neighbor Ginny, and I have no idea how he knew she likes them, but she does very much. I couldn't remember ever playing Train in his presence before, so I don't know how he recognized the album or the songs. But again, that is one of his special talents, and it won't surprise me if he is a DJ someday. He will get up and dance to movie credits; and if you want to buy him a gift, he'd rather have a gift card to download music videos than a toy. When we have people over, we hook the computer up to the TV, and he will play videos for guests for hours if you let him. Another favorite thing he does is listen to songs on his iPod in the car and add names in the lyrics. He'll be singing along to "I Gotta Feeling," and I'll hear him sing, "Tonight's gonna be a good night, Lucas, "and then just keep singing along. Or a Bieber song will go like this, "Baby, baby, baby Mitchell." He is very serious, and adding his favorite people is his favorite past time.

His other favorite is anything the big kids are doing, especially boys. If his brother is hanging out with Mitchell, then Ben is, too. Ben loves his cousin Sam, his Uncle Scott, and the neighbor who babysat him, Nate. I'm not sure if it is because he looks up to these guys, or he thinks they are cool, which of course they are, or because they all love video games. Ben *loves* all video games, whether it be on the Wii, the Xbox, the Computer, the iPad, an iPod or a Nintendo DS. Unfortunately, he will often get himself stuck on certain levels and needs his brother to "save" him over and over, but that could also be another ploy for attention.

His other fun mate is the dog, Max, or as Ben calls him "Fluffy Max." They are two peas in a pod. They bicker like siblings. Ben will annoy the dog, so the dog will wrestle with him or take his shoe and run, then Ben will cry and tell. Max is a Golden Retriever, but is big as a moose, who thinks he is a lap dog. It is not unusual for me to walk into the living room and find all three of the boys snuggled on the couch. They are all growing so fast that one of these days that couch is going to collapse beneath them. But then they will giggle like crazy.

Ben has a lot of fun, loves to entertain and dance around to make people laugh. He has acquired several musical instruments over the years, like a keyboard, an electric guitar, microphones and a little drum machine. But I think my favorite is his harmonica that he hums on all over the house. He compares himself to Justin Bieber when he has long hair; and when he has short, he will sing, "Wish I was your boyfriend" daily, and let everyone know, "I rock." Yes, yes you do.

Lucas and Ben in the pool.

Ben listening to music as usual.

Ben and his buddy Max.

Chapter Thirteen
Kee

"Kee's my best friend."
For years Ben has called Lucas "Kee". Probably because we call him Lukie, although at 14 and six foot one it doesn't quite seem to fit anymore. He's so grown, but he has always been wiser than his years.

I personally can't blame Ben for thinking Lucas hangs the moon because frankly, Tony and I think so, too. He's amazing. You're not going to believe this, but the kid does chores without being asked; he doesn't get mad very often; he says please and thank you; he helps carry in groceries; he rarely complains about anything. He's just not a normal kid. He gets good grades, does his homework without being told, cleans his room and brushes his teeth without reminder. I told you, those first two years of constant crying were like he got it all out of his system. Since then we have been blessed with an amazing, generous, thoughtful kid.

If our world seems to revolve around Ben, Ben's world revolves around Kee. Lucas is his idol, and anything Lucas does Ben must follow. This has pros and cons, of course. Lucky for us, Lucas makes a great role model. When Ben is at his most stubborn, refusing to do what is asked (like every day), 99 percent of the time, if Lucas asks him to do it, he will. Getting dressed in the morning, putting on his shoes, taking his medicine—all things Ben hates to do for Tony or me, but he will easily do for Lucas. I've learned to take the path of least resistance, which often means whatever gets the kid to do what we need him to do, let's do it. And many times that includes Lucas.

We try to keep an eye on Lukie's patience level and give him space when he needs it. Even though he is very responsible and mature, we know he also needs his time to be a kid, a teenager. So we appreciate the help he gives us with Ben, but we also try to give him opportunities for time alone and time away. That might be hanging with a friend or spending the weekend at Grandma's, whatever he needs. We all have our overload moments and try to respect each other's need for quiet. If one of us is on overload, the other two will kick in to give a break because we can all relate to how the other feels. So many times I have heard compliments from family members, other parents and teachers about Lucas. They comment about how patient he is, how kind, how calm. They notice what a good brother he is to Ben. At times, Lucas will talk to me about being around friends and how those friends bicker constantly with their siblings. I laugh and tell him that is normal, just not in our house.

From the beginning, we have included Lucas as a partner in caring for Ben. Originally this was not because we wanted him to take care of Ben. It was because as a big brother, we wanted him to have a role and a purpose and not be jealous of a younger sibling. That has actually gone very well. While Ben seems to hog and demand attention, or just require time and energy for school or behavior or doctor visits, we have never heard Lucas complain that he isn't in the spotlight. We do try to let him know when we do things for him that we are not doing for Ben, as a reminder of how he has earned more for being older or responsible. This might include driving him long distances to attend awesome summer camps where he gets to fly a plane, make glass art or build Lego Robotics. But we feel it is worth it to reward him for his conscientiousness and hard work, as well as developing his intelligence and creative opportunities.

One of our bigger concerns is that Lucas will be Ben's caretaker someday. I'm sure they will both outlive us; and while Ben may have decent independence, Lucas will need to be his guardian when we are gone, and he won't have us as his tag team. I suspect there will be other great people in Ben's life who will help Lucas, like his cousins and his friends; but I also pray that God continues to shine on my boys to give them what they need all of their days, especially when we are not here to help.

Chapter Fourteen
How Bad Does He Have It?

"How bad does he have it?"

This is the most common question I get from people when they learn Ben has DS. I don't know what specifically they are asking or how I should answer. Are they asking: how disabled is he? Do parents of kids with autism or cerebral palsy get these questions? Are they asking if he's "retarded"? If he's going to die? If he's "normal"?

There is a tendency to want to quantify the level of a disability. I get that. I want it, too. How long will he live? How much will he learn? How independent will he be? Actually, I want answers like this on *all* life topics. Who doesn't? Will things get better? Will we live to old age? Will bad things happen? I think it is the human condition to try and figure out the unknown and prepare for it, just in case. In counseling my clients, this topic comes up all the time. "What if?"

I once saw the famed psychologist Albert Ellis speak, and he said, "Don't underestimate your ability to handle adversity." So when someone asks what if, I respond, "What if it does?"

Plan for it. Often the anticipation of something happening is worse than the thing itself. People may think they couldn't handle parenting a disabled child, but if they had to, they could and they would. So when people want to know how disabled Ben is, I wonder, does it matter? Would it change anything? If I answered, "Oh he's got it BAD," would that influence their reaction? Or if I said, "Well, you can hardly tell at all," would they breathe a sigh of relief?

The truth is, as I have stated before, and as I see every day, there are no guarantees. If a child is born healthy, there is no guarantee they will stay that way. If Ben is mildly disabled now, technology or medicine may allow him to function quite "normally" in the future. Who really knows?

How bad does he have it...compared to what, to whom? Other kids with DS? Kids without DS? Your kid? My other kid? Compared to my expectations before he was born, since he was born? I actually find myself answering in such a way that puts the other person at ease. I downplay the difficulty, the hardship. I focus on our blessings. "Well, compared to some, we are lucky actually." I'm not sure if I do this to avoid pity or to shorten the uncomfortable conversation, but it works both ways because their answer is usually "Oh good." For the record, here's the honest answer.

When we first learned of his diagnosis, we were shocked. Everything we expected in the future shifted, and we had no idea what to expect. We feared for ourselves, for Ben and for Lucas. Quickly, however, after two days in the ICU, seeing one pound babies and babies with terminal illnesses and grieving parents, we knew it could be worse. So immediately things were put in perspective. Within the first year, we learned what he could have, what he did have and what he didn't. What I think of often, however, is the chicken and egg question. How much of what affects Ben's health and development is due to Down Syndrome, and how much would he have had anyway? It really doesn't matter, but it helps me keep in mind that with or without DS, he might have health and development concerns. For example, Ben has a history of ear infections and allergies and some mild asthma, but so do half of the Merz Family. Ben has HypoThyroidism, but so does my dad. Many people with DS have significant heart issues, wear glasses and have hearing aids. Ben does not.

I read once that males with DS are infertile, but females are not. I have no idea if this is true. I was told Ben would never drive a car, which worries me because we live in a rural area, without public transportation. But today I saw the second article in a year showing a DS teenager getting his driver's license.

A special education professional once told me that Ben would only develop to the equivalent of a third grader. I have no idea what that means. Will he read at a third grade level or act with the maturity of a 9 year old or what? And which nine year old? He struggles to read and write at the level of his peers; but give this kid some technology, and he figures it out with no guidance. Seriously, he can work a computer or an iPad or an iPhone, and his dad cannot. He plays video games, and his brother walks in and asks, "How did you get to this level on your own?"

The other challenge is that there are not many resources of developmental comparison that are readily accessible for DS kids. You know how the pediatrician measures your baby and tells you where they rank in height and weight? Kids with DS are generally shorter and heavier, but what is normal to expect from a DS kiddo? I know most kids walk around age one, but when do most DS kids walk? Yes he is behind, but is he ahead of what I should expect from a DS kid? No idea.

There is an average IQ in our society (85-115), but what is average IQ for a DS person? No idea. Folks, I do this for a living, and I don't know. Maybe that information is out there, and it's my responsibility to find it. But I can tell you that there is no central data base that is handed to parents to help them know "how bad" their kid has DS. Testing IQ requires an ability to read, so if a person can't, they will obviously score with a low IQ. But what if we could create a test that allowed them to be compared to their own DS peers? This should be my PhD dissertation...

So, I don't know the answer to the question, "How bad does he have it?" I know what is normal for us, and every day we adjust to what Ben is capable of. The best advice I got from any professional was—do not baby him. He thinks he can do everything, and he doesn't know what he doesn't know, which may be the best blessing of all. Because even if society expects less of him because of his diagnosis, he never expects less of himself.

Chapter Fifteen
The R Word

"You are so retarded."
"That is so gay."
"I'm going to kill you."
These are all slang words that are so commonly used in daily life, people don't generally stop to think about what they are saying or whom they are saying it to. The clinical definition of Mental Retardation, commonly called MR, is an IQ of 70 or below and indicates a person has significantly below average intelligence. (Average IQ is 85-115). Retarded can mean slow, like the plant has retarded growth.

But slang has turned the word into a slanderous description of people with DS and all people of lower functioning. People will bang their hand sideways on their chest and slur their words to be indiscernible, and the other person will know what they mean and laugh. Similarly, when someone speaks a foreign language, as a joke someone will talk slow, loud and mimic sign language. Like that's funny. Haha, not funny. But it is not often questioned because people don't listen to what they are saying. Or maybe they don't care. Where is the person that speaks up and says, hey that's not ok?

I had a *counselor* who *works for me* once say, "Oh duh, I'm so retarded." Really? Really??Are you listening to yourself? Apparently not. People will make a fat joke when they themselves are overweight. They will slander black people and be related to one. Just as professional sports teams and school mascots have gotten attention for not being politically correct regarding Native Americans, so we must pay attention to the things we say in general. I have clients who have had family members murdered, and then become sensitive to people saying "I'm going to kill you." Understandably so. The things we say become habit, and we don't even think about their true meanings.

I don't claim to be exempt. I grew up in a family that had a slanderous name for every ethnic group, and jokes were told at every holiday. Until I was an adult, I didn't know there was something wrong with that. At age 22, my African American supervisor had to write me up at work for making a prejudiced comment, and she had to explain to me what I said and why it was wrong. I was 22! And even then I didn't know until she told me. That was an eye opener.

So I understand how it is that people say these things without thinking or sometimes without knowing. Before Ben was born I don't remember using the word retarded in my vocabulary, but I don't remember being offended by it either. However once the R-word became personal, I heard it everywhere.

Listening to stand-up comedy is an interesting study of what humor is acceptable over the years. In past decades, there were far more jokes about race because people thought that was funny. Today that still happens, but the more socially acceptable jokes are about "retards, fat people and midgets." Maybe it is the human condition for people to label and create hierarchies. Maybe those who are insecure build themselves up by knocking others down. Survival of the fittest? These groups are picked on because they are easily conquered? Can't defend themselves? Whatever the excuse, I just wish people would pay attention to what they are saying. Some people are malicious, but others don't even realize what they are saying.

Luckily, more awareness is happening. The show *Glee* has had two characters with DS, a student in a wheelchair, students who are gay, a girl who is overweight, one with OCD, and a boy dealing with transgender issues. The risqué show, *American Horror Story*, has had an actress with DS as a main character for multiple seasons. The Trevor Project has made great strides in awareness and support for LGBTQ issues. And there was an excellent campaign in 2012 on TV and YouTube about "The R Word." In May 2015 a new movie called Where Hope Grows comes out starring a young man with DS. I cannot wait to see it.

So as a society, we are making strides and creating awareness, and that is awesome. Facebook helps, in my opinion. Of course I post all the time about Ben because he is a crack up. I don't do this to exploit him. Heck, I post just as much about Lucas.

But over the past few years, there are more general posts on social media celebrating DS kids in the media: DS teens being voted homecoming queen and king, getting modeling gigs, becoming the batboy for Major League Baseball teams, running the New York marathon. People post these stories on their sites, and everyone cheers, likes and shares. I know not everyone likes it or cares about it. But I love that the medium is available to create widespread awareness.

In my work, I have noticed a trend in human behavior. People are either insightful, or they're not. By that I mean, when people come to counseling to work on things, some are aware that their own thoughts and behaviors contribute to their feelings, and some people are totally unaware. An example would be a parent asking me, "Why does my little jerk of a kid not respect me?" They have no idea that the behavior they are modeling is contributing to the problem. This idea of awareness applies to many aspects of society. Take for example church-goers who do not act very Christian-like. They can recite their beliefs, but they don't put them in action in daily life. In Alcoholics Anonymous, they call this "talking the talk, but not walking the walk."

Such is the challenge regarding the topic of this chapter. Some people will become more aware and try to monitor their own words. If they use these derogatory connotations, they will now become more aware and work to eliminate them. Others will have no idea they are doing it, or have no idea how to watch for it. They simply do not have the capacity for self-awareness. I'm not being cynical. I honestly don't think some people get why this is a big deal. I suspect this has always concerned me, but it has never felt as personal as it does now. Now that it hurts me, I hear it everywhere.

On the flip side, I was inspired by a young friend of ours named Jordyn. One day at school, she came up to me and said, "Miss Merz, can I tell you something?" She was nine years old at the time. "Some kids in the hall were making fun of you and Ben [because I am overweight and Ben has DS], so I told them to shut up because Ben is my friend; and if they keep saying it, then I won't be their friend." Nine! She was nine! I love this kid.

Another day on the school bus, a teenage neighbor who had many behavior issues was calling Ben a retard and telling him to hurry up. Our teen neighbor Jodi, who was also our babysitter, told that kid to shut up; and the next day, she went to the principal who addressed it with the kid. The troubled teen, of course, denied it. But that doesn't matter.

For me, both of these stories are victories. For Ben. For us. And for society. I know there will be discrimination and ridicule. But it swells my heart with love to know there are people who stand up for what is right. There is hope. Hallelujah and Amen.

Chapter Sixteen
School

Growing up in St Louis County, Missouri, in the seventies, the school we attended was determined by where we lived. Geography dictated the "district" we attended, just like a parish determined Catholic Church and school. (Hence the St Louis tradition of asking, "Where did you go to school?" The answer slyly belied your economic status and whether we knew the same people.)

Special education was different back then. There was one "special school district" for the whole county; and depending on need, kids would be in a special ed class in their own district but taught by SSD employees, or they would attend a centrally located special ed school that could better meet the educational goals for kiddos with more significant needs. The kids who attended in my school were in the "special" class most of the day, and "mainstreaming" was rare. Negative stigma surrounded the kids who rode the "short bus," or who were in "that class." That stigma has stuck around for a long time. Even though great strides have been made in current school settings to not single out kids with special needs, parents are still reluctant to tell school officials if their child has a diagnosis because they fear their child will be treated and judged unfairly. Many hours are spent in my office educating parents about laws protecting their children and their rights in the public school system.

When Tony, Lucas, Ben and I first moved to the rural county where we live, there was a similar idea to SSD, but it was called The Co-op. There was a county central office that assessed the needs of the students, hired and trained the staff and therapists to help them and monitored progress. The benefit of the co-op, in my opinion, was that they could create specialized classes according to diagnosis. So at one school they might have a class for hearing impaired students, and all kids in the county who qualified went there. At another school there might be a Down Syndrome class and at another, an autism class. In this way, the common needs of a diagnosis could be addressed by teachers who specialized in that topic. Parents of kids with similar issues could meet and offer support. Any kid from any district could go to the central office for testing and evaluation. There was consistency between districts regardless of district resources. And then it became mismanaged and ran out of money. Shocker. SO goes the way of social service.

When the co-op disbanded, or decentralized, each school district became responsible for their own special ed students. Some of the schools coordinated efforts for early childhood. But for the most part, the district with larger populations or more affluent tax bases were able to provide better special ed services for their students. Initially, there was a race to hire the best special ed professionals in the county. So the districts who were behind the ball got the least effective teachers, and/ or the least effective teachers got the lowest paying jobs. Not very convenient for the children or their families.

The district we live in is tiny — there are 60 kids in Lucas's entire grade. When we moved here, Tony and I were concerned about whether our children would be offered a competitive education to prepare them for college. We had both grown up in the suburbs with 350 kids in our graduating class, and we went to big colleges. What we have found here now is many like-minded parents, concerned about providing quality competitive education, who also happen to work in our district and can facilitate change. Great improvements have been made in our district regarding technology, college prep and athletics, and more is on the way. We are pleased. In addition, what we didn't anticipate but love, is the small-town atmosphere. My kids walk through the halls, and everyone knows them, including the janitors and the bus drivers. It is a community that emphasizes character, while other schools are installing metal detectors.

The downside is a special education classroom that has only ten kids in it, kindergarten through eighth grade, with ten different diagnoses. There is a whole lot of love, but not a whole lot of specialization. For my household, we did not benefit by the co-op disbanding, in my opinion.

From age zero to three, Ben had First Steps, and therapists came to see him at home and at daycare. From age three to five, these services were provided through the school system, paid for by the department of education, by law. The year Ben turned three was the year the co-op ended, but our area had not yet established an early childhood center, so I was lucky enough to get Ben enrolled in an ECC near my work and near his same daycare. So even though ECC was only half a day, the bus took him back to daycare. It was a win-win. The second semester the local ECC opened closer to home, and I was in a quandary. We both worked full-time days, Lucas went to school, grandparents lived an hour away; what would we do for daycare after noon? There weren't any close to home or school. Again, here was the benefit of a small personal school; they agreed to have a bus driver drive Ben from ECC the thirty minutes out of their way to his old daycare. What a relief. What a gift!

Our district's Early Childhood Center was in a brand new building with state of the art equipment. Interactive Smart Boards and sensory rooms, and classes assigned by need like the old co-op had done. Four districts shared this ECC, so more kids attended, and specialized classes could be formed. I liked this, and I loved the staff. When Ben started, he was not very verbal, but he sure was when he finished two years later. These days the co-op kids are 100 percent mainstreamed into the district preschool, which in my opinion has pros and cons. But that could be a whole other chapter.

At the ECC, Ben had a class of six kids with a main teacher and an assistant teacher. His speech therapist, physical therapist and occupational therapist saw him at the school and were paid by the district. They helped Ben with fine motor skills, gross motor skills and speech and language through pictures as well as verbal language. They addressed behavior and educated us on what was normal and what was not. We had daily correspondence about what Ben was working on and what we could do at home. Together, we set his goals and discussed his progress. It was an excellent program. I did NOT think Ben was ready to go to kindergarten when he did. His birthday is in July, so he was a very young five when school started in the fall. But by law, if he didn't start then, he would get no services for a year. Sigh. So he went, even though he wasn't academically, developmentally or socially ready.

Before he started, I was discussing the upcoming year with a colleague, and I mentioned the teacher's name. She said, "Uh oh."
"What? Why the uh oh?"
Apparently, the teacher had a bit of a reputation in the county as not one of the better special education teachers. Great, I thought. Ben wasn't ready, and his teacher wasn't qualified. Just what we needed. I'm not sure if my preconceived notions were obvious, but I tried really hard to give her the benefit of the doubt. I smiled, I helped, I gave suggestions. But she let me know that she needed none of that. She let me know that she *never* had problems with Ben in her classroom, and maybe I should examine my parenting skills. (Not that I thought I was a perfect parent, but did she really say that out loud?)

She *did* get results from Ben—and from all of the kids. Because she was a yeller and a shamer which is *not* my style and not what my counselor instincts feel are good for kid upbringing. She rolled around the class in her desk chair, rarely getting up to do her job. She would have a student get up to retrieve something for her that was barely beyond arm's reach. She had a 7th grade special education student supervise Ben in the bathroom daily, until I brought that ethics nightmare to the principal's attention.

She loved those kids, she did. I know she did. But she had no idea how to read or utilize an IEP. And the day I walked in on her yelling at a student, "Do you want me to put you in a restraint," was the day I had had enough. Luckily for us, and for Ben, there was a guardian angel across the hall.
Mrs. Block is the kindest, most upbeat kindergarten teacher you could meet. She teaches in the same classroom she attended kindergarten in, and she loves every one of those kiddos. She talked to Ben daily at lunch, and they became friends. When it was time for Ben to repeat kindergarten (because let's face it, the first year did not count), we requested he spend half of his time in her classroom. When the "team" creates a student's IEP, they determine how many minutes the child gets in the resource room, with the therapists, and with the main classroom.

Ben loved Mrs. Block's class. He was not perfect, that's for sure, but her gentle, firm ways, coupled with all of his new friends, taught him so much that we decided to do it again, one more time, the next year. He learned so much the second year. Not as much as his peers, but he had learned the routine and the structure, and we suspected he would just add to it by doing it again, one more time. And we were right. The other benefit was that her classroom was directly across the hall from the special ed class, so there was less chance of Ben escaping out the front door. Mrs. Block was a God-send. Even now Ben walks by her class and says, "Hey Block!" in his deep voice, and she high fives him right back.

I was not sad one bit when there were district cuts and changes the next year, and that mean, ole teacher had to roll on her merry way. Ben's new teacher Ms. Dickey had experience, knowledge and patience. Never did I hear her yell. She communicated with me. She was firm at the times she needed to be and gentle and creative at others. She had curriculum ideas that were individualized for Ben, and she was always trying something new to engage him. He pushes the limits, for sure, and there are days he exhausts her. But we are very grateful she is his teacher. She also has some great classroom assistants who go the extra mile. Again, a community has made a difference for Ben.

In first grade, Ben spent half the time in the classroom and half in Dickey's class, and the same for second grade. The academics are becoming a challenge; and while he LOVES to socialize, he also gets bored and starts getting into everyone's business. Ben does not like the same old routine, which school often is. So we are currently in the process of shifting some of his "minutes" so that he has more individualized instruction and can learn at his own pace while still being challenged. Ms. Dickey has done a great job of incorporating technology into his education because she knows that motivates him.

On a final note, living in a rural community does hinder us at times. There are some unique educational opportunities for kids with DS in the St. Louis area that I'd love to enroll Ben in. Things like a six week special reading instruction class for DS kids. But my kids are not tolerant of super busy go-go-go routine and this would mean a lot of driving. They need their down time, so sometimes we miss cool opportunities by living out here. But the pros outweigh the cons so far, so we stay.

Ben can legally stay in public school until he is 21 and probably will. He will likely not repeat any more grades because most of his academic work will be done individually, but he will participate with his peers in things like music, gym, art and electives. People ask if I want Ben to be in the main classroom 100 percent of the time. My initial answer was that wouldn't be good for the group; but our advocate informed me it is not up to me to worry about the others, Ben has the *right* to be in there. But I'm not sure it is in *anyone's* best interest. Our educational goal for Ben is for him to continue learning as much as he can toward independence. We want him to be able to communicate effectively with others and function in daily life. We want him to read enough to get where he needs to go, do math enough so someone doesn't screw him out of his change and behave well enough so that he can interact with people without being a burden. Ben wants to do everything other kids do; and so far, he sees no reason why he can't. We hope he functions well enough that he can do anything he sets his mind to.

Chapter Seventeen
Technology

One morning on the way to school, Ben asked for my phone to play music because he knows mine is the one that plays through the car speakers via Bluetooth, and he likes everyone to hear his selections. He's a celebrity like that. He scrolls through the phone until he finds a song he likes and plays it, and we are surprised daily by what he chooses. I often find myself asking, "Where did you find that song? That's on my phone?"

This kid can't yet read, but he can deliberately find a song he is looking for. Sometimes it's from the album artwork, but he can also open an album and choose the song he wants from a list of 24. How does he do that? I have no idea.

Gadgets are a hobby of mine, so we have fun technology all over our house. The irony is that Tony is so old school he rarely even uses an ATM card. He can; he just doesn't. He doesn't record or pause TV; he doesn't text; he doesn't use online banking; and he still carries a sleeve of 50 CDs to play in his car. I am constantly asking him to let me make him an iPod playlist or download an eBook for him. Nope. But Ben, since age 3, has had a natural talent. He is drawn to technology of any kind. He pushes the buttons on the pin pad at the grocery store; he picks up every landline phone he finds to talk on; he finds a way to Skype or use Netflix even if I hide the apps. He loves it.

So we keep technology available. He has access to iPods, iPhones, iPads, desktop computers, laptop computers and touch screen computers. He plays his Nintendo DS, the Wii and the Xbox. He loves the online game Minecraft, because Lukie does, and Lukie is a god. My friends will tell you this is my excuse to buy more gadgets; but in addition to that, it is another way to get info into Ben's head. Of course, sometimes using technology backfires, like the time he decided to cook macaroni in the microwave without water and scorched it. But he improvised and made himself a jelly sandwich instead.

As stated earlier, we had to move the garage door button higher because he learned how to get out, and now he even stacks things so he can climb up. Luckily he knows how to input the code to get back in also. We installed locks high on the inside of our house doors because he was escaping, but he learned to move furniture to climb up, and now is tall enough to open it faster than I can. When it is something he wants to do, he is determined. One week he was home with an ear infection, and Lucas came home from school to find his laptop on and the screen rearranged. He had to system restore to fix it.

In the classroom, they now have Smart Boards. If you haven't seen them, they are amazing. Instead of a chalkboard, the wall is covered in a movie screen that links to the computer. It is also a touch screen, so kids can interact with it. This is amazing for kids with sensory issues, learning issues, motor skill and language delay. It's a whole different avenue for communication, and Ben is a master. He struggles with holding a pencil because his fingers are short, and he is easily frustrated. But lucky for him, technology is allowing him to touch and type to get his information across. I do want him to learn to write, but it is a relief to know that there are ways he can communicate with others to get his needs met, which is our number one goal for him.

The other day, as we were driving in the car (every drive is a long one when you live in the country), my sister-in-law Tina told the boys, "In the old days, we didn't get to watch movies and play on iPads in the car. We just looked out the window." I don't think they heard her through their headphones.

Just like in many families today, we have to encourage moderation. Tony is fond of saying, "That stuff will rot your brain." So we make sure they get outside and run around and play or build something or use their imaginations.

Luckily, though, Ben's love for his technology gives us an advantage in discipline. He used to not understand the warnings of consequences, but he does now. So we will tell him the game is going into time out if he doesn't comply with what is asked (usually getting ready for school in the morning). It is also a means of reward. He has a wallet, and he likes dollars, so those are his rewards for things like taking his medicine and being a good listener at school. He *loves* WalMart; so even if he hasn't earned enough to buy a new video game, just going to the store is a joy for him and something we can get him excited about as the week goes on. He *is* the kid, though, that would run past the bank of stereos on display and turn the volume up on every one, just because he can. He's a boy, and he loves buttons and things that go beep. We know that we cannot leave him in the car because I am sure he believes he could drive it; and actually he probably could, if his short little legs could reach.

Chapter Eighteen
Planning For the Future

Every parent wonders and worries about their children's future. Will they be successful? Will they graduate and be able to make it on their own? Will they live at home until they are 40? The worries are no different with a disabled child, but things we took for granted had to shift. We cannot assume he will drive or live alone. It is possible, but not guaranteed. Currently there are programs that may hire him as an adult, but who's to say these will still be around 20 years from now. At this point, if the community and the economy don't change dramatically and deny services to the disabled, his future has many options. He will graduate from high school with a diploma, and he will go to a college program that will teach him life skills and independence. He has had a caseworker since birth and will have one through adulthood, barring loss of government programs in that area. This person will assist us in knowing where there are independent living options, job and school options, and how to access income and insurance when he needs them. If Tony and I are no longer living, they can assist Lucas as part of Ben's team.

Where we would have expected to save for college, we now save for the care of Ben. We have been blessed by friends and family members who have let us know that they will be available to help in the care of Ben's future. Wow. That is generosity that is difficult to give appropriate thanks. How do you thank someone for putting your mind at ease? That is invaluable.

When Ben was in the hospital at the beginning of his life, I visited every day and had lunch in the cafeteria every day. I would often see people with disabilities working in the dining room, cleaning tables, arranging chairs, greeting customers. They were cheerful; they were proud, and they were respected. I suspect there is a department in the hospital that hires and manages the people with disabilities because there were quite a few. Seeing them during the time when I had no idea what my son's future held made my heart swell with hope and joy. I saw these folks living a normal life and working alongside coworkers who respected them, and I knew that Ben could have that someday. This image has stayed with me all of these years as a beacon of how much potential Ben really has.

There are specialists who help parents do financial planning for kids with disabilities. It is a unique situation, and as Ben gets older the questions and concerns we have change. We used to wonder when he would walk, now we wonder when he will slow down.

Every year brings something new to learn and think about. Lucas recently commented that watching Ben every day reminds him slow down and not take things for granted. While most of us breeze through every day routines, each step can be a chore for Ben that he must repeat over and over. It's no wonder he gets frustrated and shuts down sometimes. Who wouldn't?

I started this book writing about the Rock Star who is Ben, but have come to realize that the other hero here is Lucas. He doesn't know any other life, one without a disabled brother. This is his "normal" also, and I am not exaggerating, he never complains. He gives and he cares selflessly. He has a huge future ahead of him. He is gifted with intelligence, responsibility and conscientiousness and we have no doubt he will be a success.

At times I worry about where Ben will end up, who will take care of him, where he will live. But I am reminded of daycare, when I worried he couldn't make it in the toddler class. If his pattern proves consistent, it will be Ben taking care of Lucas and us, not the other way around.

Such is life with a rock star and a superhero.

Acknowledgements

We could not do this alone. There are so many people that in just these few years have made a huge impact on Ben's life and our own. Some work behind the scenes, and some are put in the spotlight by Ben because he thinks they rock.

Initially it was hospital staff who were amazing angels, and we have no idea how they do what they do every day. Then it was the in-home staff who started therapy from day one until now: the First Steps program, St. Louis Regional Center and especially Susan Baker who has been our guide and expert through this process. We are thankful for the therapists whose eternal patience taught Ben so much and help him grow and develop, especially Gina Whitener his COTA, and Megan McGinnis his speech therapist at school.

School staff have been amazing…and patient. All the staff at his preschool WeeCare, but most especially Miss Donna, Miss Diane and Mr. Ryan, we are thankful for. The whole place is amazing; all of his teachers have been amazing, and I recommend the place to everyone. At Grandview, his special ed teacher Ms. Dickey works so hard to get creative to teach Ben when he doesn't want to learn, and the principal Mrs. Bequette who continues to be patient with Ben even when he pushes her buttons and gives her a heart attack. And most especially Mrs. Block who has been Ben's friend and teacher.

I want to sincerely thank Dr. Steven Mueth, Ben's pediatrician, and his staff. Dr. Mueth has become an expert in DS, and nothing seems to phase him. He always encourages me to call if I have questions, he doesn't get annoyed when I ask more than once, and he always seems to be right. I trust him implicitly with the care of my children, and the fact that he was The Billiken (Saint Louis University mascot) makes him that much cooler.

Our circle of friends has been nothing but loving and encouraging. They have taught their children to include Ben and communicate with Ben, and they themselves hug all over Ben. We are very grateful for two amazing babysitters, Jodi Mueller and Nathan Phelps, who spent hours with Lucas and Ben after school, patiently convincing him every single day to get in the car at the bus stop, watching way more hours of SpongeBob and video games than they'd ever want to again, and never ever complaining at how little we paid them for the great job they did. Plus Jodi even arranged for Santa to visit our house!

In the friend category, I have to mention the Zophs because they have taught their kids to respect Ben, include Ben, and stick up for Ben. Mitchell is Lucas's best friend, but don't tell Ben that because he thinks Mitchell and Jordyn belong to him. To Ginny and Mike Phelps, our neighbors and our friends who love our kids like their own. They are the people we call when no one can get the kids from the bus, when we need a favor, or when we can't find Ben! They are always there for us, and they never say no. In my head, I have a list of all the things they have done for us, and I know I can never repay them. They are givers, and *some people* are just awesome like that.

And then there is family. In my work I meet so many people who don't have good family, and I am continually reminded of what a miracle we have in family. Our families are not perfect, and they don't always get along nor do the right thing, but there is no doubt the depth of their love.

I want to thank my dad and Robert for creating opportunities for my kids to travel, see fun places and make great memories; for providing a foundation of a financial future for Ben and for combining Christmas gifts one year to buy the kids a trampoline that has gotten endless use for years since.

I am grateful that my kids are close to their aunts and uncles and cousins. I grew up with an amazing extended family whom I still have fun with, and I'm so glad my kids get this, too. Sandy and Louis, Emily, Allison and Logan Hagene, Susan and Ryan McCrea, so many good times. My brother Scott and "ZZ" and especially cousin Sam Thompson who is one of Ben's all time favorite people. Tina Merz, whom Tony and I got to see grow up, now returns the favor to my children by always being there when we need her and being the favorite aunt. From kickball to marching band, from video games to being the only other person who knows how to bribe Ben, we love you so much and thank you for all of your help. Tony's parents, Rich and JoAnn Merz, who will do anything for us, any time. They will drop everything they are doing to babysit or come pick up the kids. They will drive an hour for a thirty-minute concert. They are supportive and generous and never complain even when we ask their help over and over.

"PooPoo Brad" and my mom also go above and beyond for the grandkids. Brad has turned out to be the most patient, creative Grandpa I'd ever want for my kids. Who knew you could play Bob the Builder for three hours straight? And my Mom, Marilyn Thompson, who has been my rock, who reads me like a book, who loves us all unconditionally. Mom has been there through thick and thin, cries when I cry, but can always make us laugh with silliness. I had the best memories of my grandma growing up, and I know my kids will, too.

I cannot live this life without Tony and Lucas and Ben. I once said that Lucas is the pin around which our family turns. He is the calming factor. Everyone loves him. Ben has an energy, but Lucas does, too. Our little family is a team, a unit, and my happy place is right at home with them because there is really nothing better.

Ben looking in Santa's ear when he came to visit.

The four of us, 2007

My friend Tracy Zoph asked me to include this picture because we got such a kick out of it. This is Lucas, Mitchell and Ben with the band teacher. But compare Ben in the front to Tony in the left background. Mini-me. Spring 2014.

Resources

National Down Syndrome Society (US)
http://www.ndss.org/

Down Syndrome Association of Greater St. Louis
http://dsagsl.org/

NIH definition of Trisomy 21
http://www.nlm.nih.gov/medlineplus/ency/article/000997.ht
m

Babies With Down Syndrome, A New Parent's Guide
http://www.amazon.com/dp/1890627550/ref=sr_ob_2?ie=UTF
8&qid=1428550295&sr=8-2

Sensory Processing Disorder
http://spdfoundation.net/about-sensory-processing-disorder/

The Out of Sync Child by Carol Kranowitz
http://out-of-sync-child.com/

Central Auditory Processing Disorder
https://www.understood.org/en/learning-attention-
issues/child-learning-disabilities/auditory-processing-
disorder/auditory-processing-disorder-what-youre-seeing

TASK Sports (Team Activities for Special Kids)
http://www.tasksports.org/

Moving Mountains Counseling, LLC
http://www.movingmountainscounseling.com/

About The Author

Amie Merz is a Licensed Counselor in private practice helping families help themselves. While her Master's Degree prepared her well for counseling others, it has been the life experiences that have taught her the most. She, her husband and her two sons live in the country south of St. Louis, Missouri.

Smoky Mountains, Spring 2015

www.ingramcontent.com/pod-product-compliance
Lightning Source LLC
LaVergne TN
LVHW051745080426
835511LV00018B/3236